THE COMPLETE GUIDE TO BERNESE MOUNTAIN DOGS

Andrea Brown Berman

Publication Data

Bernese Mountain Dogs
The Complete Guide to Bernese Mountain Dogs – First edition.
Summary: "Successfully raising a Bernese Mountain Dog from puppy to old age" –
Provided by publisher.
ISBN: 978-1-952069-78-9
[1. Bernese Mountain Dogs – Non-Fiction] I. Title.

This book has been written with the published intent to provide accurate and authoritative information in regard to the subject matter included. While every reasonable
precaution has been taken in preparation of this book the author and publisher expressly
disclaim responsibility for any errors, omissions, or adverse effects arising from the use or
application of the information contained inside. The techniques and suggestions are to be
used at the reader's discretion and are not to be considered a substitute for professional
veterinary care. If you suspect a medical problem with your dog, consult your veterinarian.
Design by Sorin Rădulescu
First paperback edition, 2020

Cover Photo Courtesy of Calli Borutski
Dog's name: Belle, IG: @belle.andfriends

TABLE OF CONTENTS

CHAPTER 12

CHAPTER 13

CHAPTER 14

CHAPTER 15

CHAPTER 20

INTRODUCTION

E veryone loves a Bernese Mountain Dog. How could you not? The list of their attributes is long: they're cute, cuddly, intelligent, and most commonly categorized as "those big, fuzzy, Teddy-bear dogs". They turn heads wherever they go, and they rarely fail to elicit an overwhelming desire to take one home and make him your next best buddy. But wait. Before you seek out that perfect shaggy canine companion, there are a few things (actually, many things) to consider. A Berner may seem like the perfect dog, but is it the perfect dog for you?

As with most breeds, there are plusses and minuses, and we hope that as you read further in this book, you'll gain the knowledge to make an informed decision as to whether you (and those in your household) are ready to take on the responsibilities that this breed requires. If you are contemplating adding a dog to your household, you are making a major commitment. It's not a commitment that should be taken lightly and without an enormous amount of consideration as to what may lie ahead.

Photo Courtesy of Andrea Berman

So, what, exactly, DOES lie ahead? The pleasure of caring for a giant dog with a giant heart who will love you unconditionally for his entire life. The joy of watching a puppy grow into a mature dog who will bring you years of happiness. If you're thinking about adding an older Berner to your household, you'll have the comfort of knowing that you're providing him with a new, loving, fur-ever home.

In addition to all those positives, there could be a few "speed bumps" along this "Berner Highway". Bernese Mountain Dogs don't live as long as some other breeds. They are known to have health issues, veterinary costs can be expensive, and some owners find that their dog's shedding can become a daily house-cleaning task.

Photo Courtesy of Andrea Berman

As an owner of a Bernese Mountain Dog and as a professional dog trainer, I'm here to offer my perspective from both sides of the Berner spectrum and to give you the tools you'll need to successfully welcome this amazing breed into your home and heart. There's no breed quite like a Bernese Mountain Dog. Read on to find out why!

CHAPTER 1

The ABCs of the Bernese Mountain Dog

Affectionate

These gentle giants are considered by many to be the living, breathing version of the plush stuffed animal that you snuggled up with as a child. If you're looking for an oversize lap dog to keep you warm on a frigid winter night, this may be your pup.

Breeder

There are great breeders, mediocre breeders, and breeders who won't hesitate to take your hard earned money in exchange for a dog which may

Photo Courtesy
of Nick Timmerman

ultimately cost you an exorbitant amount in veterinary bills. If you're plan-ning to purchase a Berner from a breeder, here's our best advice: do your homework and find a reputable breeder.

Cold weather
BMDs originated in the mountains of Switzerland. They love nothing better than chilly days and a good romp in the snow. Hot, humid climates are not the best choice for a Bernese Mountain Dog.

Drool
While BMDs are not top on the list of dogs most likely to salivate all over your elegant white upholstered chair, some Berners are worse droolers than others. Typically, most have dryer mouths, but the potential is always there.

Exercise
A Bernese Mountain Dog can be fairly high energy and needs plenty of physical as well as mental stimulation. A large fenced-in yard, several long walks a day, and plenty of room to play will make for a happy dog. Berners were bred to be working dogs. Without the means to expend some energy, this breed has been known to create plenty of mischief.

Family
Berners are the ultimate family dog. They are gentle and loving, devoted and loyal, bond well with both adults and children, and are amaz-ing guardians of their human pack. Their sweet demeanor makes them excellent companions.

Grooming
They shed. A lot. A thorough brushing once a week plus a visit to a professional groomer three or four times a year should, in most cases, be sufficient.

Healthy
Not so much. Unfortunately, Berners are prone to a larger number of disorders than many other breeds. Hip and elbow dysplasia, cancer, bloat, joint and muscle issues, skin allergies, and eye and ear problems are com-mon in Bernese Mountain Dogs.

Isolation
BMDs are not happy when left alone for long periods of time. A lonely, bored Berner has the potential to wreak havoc in your home. These dogs need the company of their pack to thrive.

Jobs
A Bernese Mountain Dog loves to work. At the appropriate age, physical stamina, and with proper training, this breed can pull a cart, carry a back-pack, and has the potential to become a wonderful therapy dog.

Klutz
As youngsters, BMDs are not usually considered the most graceful breed of dog. Until they mature, they can be quite clumsy and awkward. You may want to put away that delicate heirloom vase until your Berner puppy is a bit more physically coordinated.

Life expectancy
BMDs, like many giant dog breeds, typically have a shorter life expectancy. Seven to ten years is average.

Maturity
This dog is known to be somewhat slower to mature, both physically and mentally, than other breeds. You may wonder why your two or three-year-old BMD is still acting like a puppy and hasn't settled down yet. He will. Eventually.

Novice owners
It's imperative that a first-time dog owner research and learn as much about this breed as possible before adding a Berner to the human family. Forewarned is forearmed. They are wonderful pets as long as you have the necessary knowledge along with realistic expectations.

Obedience training
Big dog + bad doggy manners can spell trouble. A well-trained Bernese is a joy to behold.

Patient, peaceful, playful, and powerful
See above - Obedience training.

Quiet
Most Berners are not known to be obnoxious barkers. However, they will certainly let you know if something is amiss or if someone's at the door.

Responsive
Bernese Mountain Dogs are smart. They will quickly figure out which members of the family are the "Alpha Dogs". While we're at it, let's add a few more "R" words to the equation. It will be your Responsibility to teach your Berner Respect for every member of his human pack, young or old.

Sociable
The Berner loves his family, does well with other dogs and usually cats, and needs early exposure to a variety of people, places, and things. Encourage him to safely explore his surroundings as well as people and pets outside of his pack.

Tireless
Your BMD puppy may seem like he has boundless energy. However,

it's important to keep him at an even pace. Too much exercise can have an adverse effect on a young pup's growing bones and physical structure.

Underdog
Rare is the BMD with an inferiority complex. These dogs are confident, courageous, clever, and charming...did we mention cute?

Veterinary visits
Addressing health concerns in a timely manner and staying up to date on check-ups for your BMD is essential. Your veterinarian should be considered a lifelong investment in your dog's health and well-being.

Watch dogs
Berners are excellent watch dogs. Generally speaking, although they are not considered to be aggressive, they know when to step in to protect their own.

EXpenses
A giant breed dog has giant expenses: health issues, obedience training, toys, grooming, doggy day care and/or dog sitters, start-up supplies (beds, food bowls, crates, etc.). These costs can break the bank, so know what you'll need to budget before you commit to pet parenthood.

You
Such a small word but such an essential part of your relationship with your Bernese. YOU will ultimately be the one responsible for the life of your dog. Are you prepared to ensure your Berner's care, feeding, safety, and happiness for years to come? He will trust you, protect you, and be a faithful and loving companion. Can you promise your Berner the same?

Zany
These dogs are also goofy, rambunctious, happy-go-lucky, comical, curious, intelligent, snuggly, good-natured, patient, friendly, loving, and an over-all great companion. The Berner may seem like the perfect dog, but is it the perfect dog for you? Let's find out!

CHAPTER 2
Get Acquainted with the Bernese Mountain Dog

It's difficult, if not impossible, to ignore a Bernese Mountain Dog. Its size alone is enough to make even non-dog lovers take notice. Observing that great, lumbering hulk of a canine is sheer magic in motion. It's a winning combination: a thick, tri-colored coat, an impish twinkle in those endearing brown eyes, a non-stop wagging tail, and a personality that's totally irresistible. It's the perfect combination of attributes for a dog that promises to command a colossal piece of your heart.

Photo Courtesy
of Hana Sedlmayr

Photo Courtesy of Katie Walther

Is a Bernese Mountain Dog the Right Dog for You?

"If you are a competitive obedience or agility person, you might want to think twice about a Berner. You'll likely never be out-scoring those Goldens and Border Collies. Berners are not precise. If, like most us, you are just pleased to qualify and earn our various titles, you'll enjoy working with a Berner. I call us 'green ribbon people'. In our signature event, Carting or Drafting, Berners do quite well. Speed and precision are not important, but cooperation and willingness are."

BARB WALTENBERRY

Barberry BMD

Just as every human is unique, the same holds true for every dog. There is no "one-size-fits-all" in the world of Berners, and pet parents can either take credit or blame for many of the reasons why a dog turns out the way he does. Are you a patient, laid-back, friendly type of individual, who is willing to train your dog to be the best he can be? If so, then chances are good that your Bernese Mountain Dog will mature into an easy-going, friendly companion; one who has a natural desire to please.

Your dog's genetics also play a significant role in whether your BMD matures into a happy, loving, devoted pet, or a stubborn, sullen curmudgeon. Yes, that Bernese Mountain Dog may be a fabulous example of what a breed standard should look like, but even in the doggy world, looks can be deceiving. With commitment, patience, knowledge, and lots of love, your Berner journey will prove to be an amazing adventure!

Personality and Common Characteristics

"Berners love to be the center of their family's universe. The best family would be one that would include their Berners in as many activities, outings, and gatherings as possible. They love people and attention and they do not do well as an outdoor dog, or a dog left in a kennel all of the time."

ROBIN WORTS
Swiss Destiny Bernese Mountain Dogs

Bernese Mountain Dogs possess the overall appearance and attitude of a big, goofy, happy, tail-wagger who is mainly interested in having a ton of fun. Most are eager to explore their world, ready to embark on an exciting new endeavor, or hop into the car at a moment's notice. A game of fetch? A long walk? Doggy park? C'mon! Let's go! They are enthusiastic sidekicks, with a zest for life and a willingness to venture into the unknown. A confident, trusting, loyal breed, Berners thrive on being the center of your world. They are responsive, fairly easy to train, and sensitive to the moods of their human pack members. Plus, BMDs are excellent with kids, but because this is a giant of a dog, caution should be taken around small children and older, frail adults. The Berner's gentle nature is one of the most celebrated reasons for their popularity as a family pet. They have a calm demeanor, and above all, love to be loved.

Along with all of those wonderful qualities, there are also drawbacks: some Berners can become extremely attached to a certain family member and may bond more strongly with that one particular person. Some can be aloof or shy and timid around strangers. Male BMDs, especially, can display dominant traits, most commonly toward other male dogs. Although they are happy to assume a favorite pose as a "bear-skin rug", they do require a great deal of exercise. Because they are so devoted to their human family, Berners are prone to

FUN FACT
Bernese Mountain Dog Club of America (BMDCA)

The Bernese Mountain Dog Club of America (BMDCA) was formed in 1968 and was officially granted sanctioned status by the American Kennel Club (AKC) in November 1973. The BMDCA offers breeder referrals, hosts annual events, and offers a variety of resources for Bernese Mountain Dog owners, breeders, and enthusiasts.

*Photo Courtesy
of Andrée-Anne Frigon*

separation anxiety. When excluded from your plans, your Bernese will let his disappointment be known. In that case, he may revert in his training and exhibit newly acquired bad habits, such as digging, jumping, ignoring commands, barking, and howling when left alone. When positive, consistent training is begun early, there is less of a chance that you will experience any of these behaviors.

Physical Characteristics

"Berners are low energy dogs compared to more athletic ones such as Labs. They love to run and play hard for a short while but then often prefer to come sit by your side. This is due in part to their stocky size."

DANIEL MERCER
Mermac Kennel

There's no doubt that Berners are beautiful - and big. The average weight for a male BMD is between 70 and 120 pounds. Females are usually a bit smaller, tipping the scales at between 65 and 110 pounds. Both sexes have a lifespan of roughly 7-10 years. Their bodies are sturdy, full, and strong. A blaze of white on the face, neck, and chest gives the Berner a very distinct appearance, with most sporting some white on their feet as well as the tip of their tail. Their heavy coats may be slightly curly or silky and straight, and their fur displays a healthy, shiny gloss.

If anyone in the household has dog allergies, it is highly recommended that before bringing a Berner into your home (and heart) several visits be made to breeders to see if there could be any potential human health problems. Asthma, wheezing, sneezing, and other reactions should most definitely negate adding a Bernese Mountain Dog to the family dynamics. Best to find out ahead of time. A reputable breeder will likely encourage a visit by the whole family or any individual who could possibly show signs of an adverse health reaction.

Berners shed on a seasonal basis; some seasons are worse than others. Puppies have single coats until they reach the age of approximately seven months. Shortly thereafter, their heavy, double coat will come in. Shedding is worse in the spring and fall, but it is an ongoing process. In simple terms, this means that you will invariably have dog hair on your clothes, on your furniture, or even in your dinner. You will most likely vacuum, sweep, dust, and clean the contents of your humble abode more often than you could possibly imagine. However, with frequent brushing and regular grooming of your dog, the shedding will be less obvious, but we have yet to meet a BMD owner who does not bemoan the fact that with a Berner, there's dog hair... EVERYWHERE. If this is something that you find bothersome, and if you take particular pride in a spotless, dustless, pristinely dog-hair-free household, please, please, please reconsider your choice of dog breed. Berners are loving, intelligent, amazing pets, but they DO shed. Profusely!

A Brief History of the Bernese Mountain Dog

"The Bernese Mountain Dog used to be referred to as Four Eyes. The unique brows led folks to believe that they had an extra set of eyes in order to see 'ghosts'."

DIANE CALDEMEYER REID
Faraway Farms Inc.

Bernese Mountain Dogs have a long, long history which dates back more than two thousand years. The breed, originating from a type of Mastiff-like dog, was introduced to the Swiss Mountain area by invading Roman soldiers. The early ancestors to the BMDs we know today were used as farm animals working in dairies and agricultural communities. They guarded livestock, and with their immense strength and ability to pull heavy loads, they were used as draft animals in the days prior to the implementation of mechanized farming equipment. Farmers unable to afford horses also utilized this breed in transporting their ranches' dairy products. One of four similar strains of Swiss Mountain Dogs (called Sennenhunds), the Bernese eventually became more of a companion animal as ranchers and farmers modernized their production methods. According to the American Kennel Club, the breed was imported to the United States in 1907 and was officially recognized in 1937. The rest, as they say, is history, and shortly thereafter, a big, fluffy, affectionate dog captured the hearts of Americans.

That's not to say that Bernese haven't retained their love of hard work. Cart pulling is considered one of their favorite activities, and there are still Berner cart pulling competitions sponsored by some BMD clubs. Berners are "Kissin' Cousins" to the shorter-haired Swiss Mountain Dog and are often confused with this similar breed. Today, the Bernese Mountain Dog is ranked number twenty-two in popularity of the AKC's 195 breeds. For the legions of BMD aficionados, the reasons are quite clear.

Photo Courtesy
of Alexandra Hahn

CHAPTER 3

Things to Consider Before Jumping into BMD Ownership

H ave you already made up your mind that a BMD is the dog for you and your family? Maybe it seems like it would be a good fit for your living situation; you've got the space and are willing and able to make both the time and emotional commitment. However, there are a few more elements that you need to consider:

Photo Courtesy
of Tina Williams

Photo Courtesy
of Alexandra Hahn

Cost

"I tell all prospective owners to consider the price of the puppy the down payment on the life of the dog. Unfortunately, Bernese Mountain Dogs can be expensive to own with the predisposition for dysplasia, GI issues (loose stool, bloat), heart issues, immune challenges, etc. Which is why it is so important to contact your regional Bernese Mountain Dog club for their list of reputable breeders who breed for health."

STACY SLADE
Sevens Bernese Mountain Dogs

Berners are expensive. Experienced, reputable breeders will charge a fairly high price for a high-quality dog, often between $1,000 to $2,000. But remember - you get what you pay for. Acquiring the right dog is just the beginning of your expenditures. Plan on veterinary fees for inoculations, spay or neutering, regular checkups, city or town licensing, microchipping, prevention treatments for flea, tick, and heart worm, and general lab work.

Photo Courtesy
of Anna Snider

Food and Maintenance

Can you afford a quality diet for this growing dog? Supplies (which we'll discuss more in a subsequent chapter), including dog beds, crates, leashes, bowls, and toys are just a few must-have items. Add to the ever-growing list the expense of a dog trainer, as well as a pet sitter, grooming, kennel and/or doggy day care, canine health insurance, fencing for your yard, if needed, and...well, you get the picture.

> **FUN FACT**
> **Tebow Pack**
>
> Tim Tebow, American professional baseball player for the New York Mets and former professional football quarterback, and wife Demi-Leigh Nel-Peters, South African actress and model, introduced a trio of puppies into their family in March 2020. The puppies are named Paris, Kobe, and Chunk, and have been affectionately dubbed the "Tebow Pack." Paris is a Dalmatian, Kobe is a Golden Lab, and Chunk is a Bernese Mountain Dog.

Depending upon what you consider essential and how much you are willing or able to budget for this new member of your family, there are various options when thinking about purchases. It's a good idea to shop around and decide ahead of time what's at the top on your list of "must haves". Will your dog sleep just as well in a pricey designer bed, or will a less expensive one suffice? While some items are non-negotiable, concessions are possible in some cases. Consider these decisions as you would when purchasing a new car. Do you absolutely need a sunroof? Probably not. However, you do need tires and a steering wheel. Make a list and check it twice.

Permission

Aside from the cost involved, there are other key factors. If you're a renter, has your landlord given approval for a pet, and are there any breed and size limitations for a dog? Some apartment owners and condo associations have strict regulations when pets are allowed. A breeder (or a rescue organization if you're planning to adopt) may require a permission letter from management or the association board of your community.

Photo Courtesy
of Joanne Caskey

Responsibilities

"The best home for a Bernese Mountain Dog is usually a family in a home with a large fenced yard. Berners love to be with their people and are equally happy going for a walk or lounging on the couch."

ANDREA CARLSON
Singing Sands Bernese Mountain Dogs

Who will be the primary person to take care of the dog? In a single person household, it's obvious. However, with a family situation, the answer may not be so crystal clear. We've all been there: The kids want a dog. They promise to help out, but children often have short attention spans and can tire quickly of daily chores. Add to that their after-school activities, play dates, and homework, and guess who ends up with doggy detail? The time involved with jobs, household responsibilities, and shuttling the kids to their activities and appointments can add to the everyday stress and time restrictions that we all experience. Be sure that everyone is on board when it comes to agreeing to the additional responsibilities that a dog will require.

Time

If your dog's primary caregiver is at home during day or has a flexible work schedule, it's an ideal situation. However, many of us are away from the house for long stretches of time. If that's the case in your household, you will need to hire a reliable, responsible pet sitter to come in at regular intervals to take your dog out to relieve itself and to offer some quality play time for your new canine companion.

Another option is doggy day care, which is an appropriate solution for busy pet families. We'll address the ins and outs of day care later, but keep in mind that for anyone who is away from home on a regular basis or who travels, finding a pet sitter or dog day care program should be high on the list of pooch priorities.

Yes, there are so many things to think about when considering adding a Bernese Mountain Dog to your family. A little forethought will make things easier for everyone - including your new dog. In a perfect world, everything would go according to plan, but let's face it; the world is far from perfect. Have some patience, discuss the idea, do the math, and consider all of the "what ifs". If you do, your Berner will provide you with many years of happiness and miles of smiles. Plan accordingly, and those Berner wishes just may come true!

CHAPTER 4
Buying vs. Adopting

"Even though they are very big dogs, they can be great with small children and more elderly families."

AMY KESSLER
Lionheart Bernese

By now, you're probably eating, sleeping, and dreaming Bernese Mountain Dog. First, let's get to the nitty-gritty of who, what, when, where, and how this canine will enter your life, and we'll discuss the positives and negatives of acquiring your new furry kid. Are you imagining a puppy, bounding happily through a meadow filled with yellow daffodils, followed by a host of cheerful, giggling children? Oh, and is there a rainbow and a few unicorns in that picture, too? Are you a first-time dog owner, or have you previously had a beloved dog in your life? Where will your new dog be coming from? There are pros and cons for owning younger dogs vs. older dogs, and there are pros and cons for choosing breeders, rescue organizations, and shelters. Let us offer some insight.

Photo Courtesy of Stacy Barkley

Should I get a Puppy or Rescue an Older Berner?

Puppies are adorable! Totally irresistible! Every kid needs a puppy! They'll grow up together! Life will be wonderful! (There are those darned unicorns and rainbows again.) Puppies require a tremendous amount of work. They pee a lot. They poop a lot. They need to go outside to relieve themselves often. They need to be trained. You'll lose plenty of sleep, but yes, the rewards will be immeasurable - once the hard work is done.

Things to think about: If you're imagining that a puppy will be perfect for your young children, consider the age, size, and capabilities of those children. A puppy grows quickly, and that little ball of fur will soon outweigh a small child. Will your children be physically able to withstand a bouncing, seventy-pound dog who may inadvertently knock them over in a rowdy game of fetch? Puppies are energetic creatures, and although kids are too, injuries are always possible. That goes for a young dog as well as a child. You may think that a puppy can keep up with your child, but young dogs' bodies are still developing, and too much activity can cause bone and muscle trauma to a Bernese puppy.

Are you, or a member of your household, disabled, elderly, or have physical limitations? If so, a puppy zipping around the living room at the speed of light could put you at risk for a fall or worse. If you live in a colder climate (think ice and snow), would walking a dog in sub-zero or slippery conditions pose a potential hazard for you? We're not attempting to be Negative Nancy here but rather Realistic Rosie. Accidents do happen. At a certain age, our knees and backs can develop aches, pains, and other snap-crackle-and-pop-like ailments. An older dog can provide just as much loving companionship as a puppy and won't require as many trips up and down stairs nor will he need to go out as frequently.

As a cautionary note, however, an older dog will also require a commitment on your part, sometimes more so than a young puppy. Adjusting to a new home is not easy. An adult dog may need more time to become familiar with different surroundings, routines, and family schedules. Senior dogs will have unique needs and will be discussed in a later chapter.

New pet parents may be unaware of previous conditions that might have affected a dog's physical or mental health. Was the dog abused or abandoned? Was there a bonding issue? Was the animal living primarily outside? Your dog may never have had to climb stairs, been in a home where children or other pets were present, been familiar with riding in a car, or received any training whatsoever. There can be many unknown factors that will necessitate your patience, consistency, and kindness no matter the age of the dog.

Photo Courtesy
of Colleen Hondel

Animal Shelters

If you have your heart set on a pure-bred Bernese Mountain Dog, there is a chance, although a slim one, that a BMD can be found at a shelter. It's estimated that only twenty-five percent of all shelter dogs are pure bred. The reasons why a dog might be available at a shelter are many, and it's not necessarily because there is a particular problem with the dog. A dog could find its way to a shelter because of an owner's divorce, relocation, marriage, job, or death. There might be behavioral issues that an owner was unwilling or unable to address whether for financial or other reasons. Many dogs are turned over to shelters for that too-often-heard explanation, "someone developed an allergy". Circumstances can sometimes be sketchy at best. Most shelters are overcrowded with dogs and underfunded and/or understaffed, and it's often difficult to determine the exact reason why a dog is there. Luckily, shelter workers and volunteers will try their best to match a dog with a potential owner.

There are many wonderful dogs of all ages who are homeless and in shelters, awaiting their fur-ever home, so be prepared to fall in love with your future best friend. However, if a pure-bred BMD of a certain age, gender, and temperament is what you have in mind, a shelter may not be your best choice. If a Bernese-mix or a sad-eyed Shepherd would fill that empty spot on your sofa, or if that little Chihuahua decides that he'd love to come home with you, then by all means, follow your heart.

Rescue Organizations

If you're trying to decide between purchasing a dog from a breeder or visiting a shelter, there may be a suitable alternative which falls somewhere in the middle of those two choices - breed rescues. These organizations are staffed by caring, knowledgeable individuals who are dedicated to a particular breed of dog. The fees to adopt a dog from a rescue can be somewhat lower than a breeder would charge but are generally higher than a shelter. Every breed rescue organization seeks to place their dogs in the best possible situation. Many have volunteers who foster dogs in their own homes and are familiar with a dog's temperament and are aware of specific issues. If a dog is fostered in a home with young children or other pets, a foster parent will know what type of household will be best suited for that dog. Likewise, if any aggression, shyness with strangers, or other concerns have been observed, this would also be noted in placing a BMD. Dogs of all ages are fostered, so you may meet a younger dog as well as a charming senior dog; however, most rescues rarely have puppies available.

Placement fees will vary depending upon the organization as well as the dog. There could be spaying or neutering charges, vaccinations, donations, application fees, or other expenses at the time of placement.

BMD rescue organizations are located throughout the United States as well as internationally. One excellent resource is the Bernese Mountain Dog Club of America (BMDCA.org), which offers a plethora of information as well as an extensive list of regional rescue and rehoming groups dedicated to the Berner breed. Whether your dog comes from a shelter, breeder, or rescue, expect that you will be asked to submit an application. Be prepared to provide proof of home ownership or permission from a landlord. You may need to bring others who live in your household (including pets) to meet your prospective BMD. Some rescue organizations will want to check your financial credentials, and oftentimes, a home visit from a shelter/rescue/breeder representative will be required.

Some rescues have specific policies and regulations before an application is even accepted; these include knowing the minimum age of children in the household and knowing if the yard has a fence. A dog's history, temperament, activity level, age, and prospective family situation are all taken into consideration. The ultimate goal is to match the right dog with the right home. No one wants to see a dog returned for any reason that could have been avoided.

Photo Courtesy of Mary Westrick

Pet Stores – Why You Should Avoid Them

You may have noticed one option for finding that perfect dog, the pet store, has been omitted from this list. There are so many reasons NOT to purchase a pet-store pup and not a single good reason why you should. Picture this: You walk into a pet store, just to browse. There's the cutest little Bernese Mountain Dog that you've ever seen. You're in love! The employee asks if you'd like to spend some time with this adorable fur ball - no obligation to buy, of course. You take said fur ball into a ten-foot by ten-foot enclosure, and he's absolutely Mr. Right - face licks, snuggles, tail wags all accounted for. Wait...let's ask the pet store person where the puppy came from. "Oh, a wonderful breeder out in the mid-west."

Red Flag #1: That breeder was most likely a puppy mill - an unscrupulous dog factory, only in the business to make money, with not a care in the world about their dog's health, breed standards, or genetic considerations. If you're feeling the need to purchase this dog for no other reason than to free him from his tiny cage and give him a good home, well, as soon as he leaves, that cage will be filled with another puppy-mill dog.

Red Flag #2: The pet store employee will tell you that if there's any problem once you get the dog home, they will happily take him back and give you a refund. Fast forward to a week or two later. You've purchased this adorable pup. The entire family is smitten with little pet-store Rufus. The kids adore him and vice-versa; then Rufus gets sick. You take him to the vet who tells you that he has a genetic disorder or a chronic illness. Are you going to return him to the store and break your kids' hearts at losing this dog? Are you going to be responsible for extensive veterinary care? If you DO decide to return the dog, what happens to the dog? Is he sold to another unsuspecting customer? Is he sent to a shelter? Is he euthanized?

Red Flag #3: Pet store dogs are NOT necessarily less expensive than acquiring a dog from a reputable breeder. Never mind that for this week only, he's on sale or you can put him on your American Express card or pay for him in 120 easy monthly payments.

Besides the potential for an expensive, unhealthy dog with an unknown lineage, there can be - and usually are - behavioral issues. A puppy-mill dog has spent most of his young life in a dirty, cramped cage. There's been little human contact, zero socialization, and he has probably received sub-standard nourishment. Puppy mills and pet stores are in the business for one thing and one thing only - to make money. Run; don't walk - away from the pet store puppy.

Finding a Reputable Breeder

Now that you've discovered that adding a Bernese Mountain Dog to your home is not as simple as you first thought, we come to the option of purchasing that dog from a breeder. Let's look at the specific categories of breeders first. There are great breeders, mediocre breeders, and the ones who fit into the classification of "stay away from this breeder at all cost". We'll start with the great ones and determine what you'll need to look for. As with all aspects of finding the best Bernese Mountain Dog, we can't stress this one word enough: RESEARCH!

If you know of someone who is the proud pet parent of a Berner, ASK THEM QUESTIONS! Come on, now. Don't be shy. Take a good look at their dog. Does he appear to be happy and healthy? Is he well-groomed with a clean, thick, silky/wavy coat? What's his temperament? This will tell you that the owner takes loving care of their dog, both from a health standpoint as well as appearance and training. If the owner seems approachable, strike up a friendly conversation. Most Berner parents are eager to talk about their furry kids.

Ask for the name of the breeder, whether the breeder is recommended (or not), and if they would supply you with the breeder's contact information. Is the dog healthy? Are there any physical or behavioral concerns? BMD owners, themselves, are (pardon the pun) a special breed and are often in contact with other Berner owners; be sure to inquire about anyone who may have additional breeder contacts. Veterinarians are also a good source when it comes to locating a reputable breeder. Not only do they hear from their patients about who and where they acquired their dog, they may also know about breeders who should be avoided.

Another "don't" ... please refrain from purchasing a dog from the first breeder who has a dog available, unless you are absolutely confident that it's the right breeder and dog for you. Have patience – the right breeder will come along. Besides referrals from Berner owners and veterinarians, check the internet for dog breeder sites as well as breed-specific magazines and books. The American Kennel Club lists breeders with categories that include regional locations, litter availability, health certification and registrations, dog lineage, breeder experience, etc. The Bernese Mountain Dog Club of America also lists breeder information and referrals, and they maintain a database of volunteers who are happy to discuss BMDs with potential buyers.

Regional BMD clubs are an excellent source for finding recommendations of breeders. Berner sites abound on Face Book and other social media, with pages dedicated to owners sharing information about the breed. Additionally, there are other internet sites where BMD aficionados can ask about everything from breeders to temperaments to questions and concerns.

Just a word to the wise: Always use caution when posting on any internet sites or seeking advice or suggestions from owners. Not all Berner owners will agree on best practices, and the simple act of owning a Berner does not make someone an expert. Be careful!

Photo Courtesy of Jessica Foley

Types of Breeders

Within the realm of breeders, there are three specific categories: Professional breeders, hobby breeders, and "backyard breeders". Professional breeders know their breed, their dogs' lineage, their dogs' history going back generations, and are thoroughly vested in keeping their dogs' health, temperament, and overall quality up to breed standards. They may even have show dogs of their own.

Hobby breeders are dedicated, knowledgeable individuals who may produce a smaller number of litters and who may work toward maintaining a particular lineage of dogs. They are no less professional than a good, reputable breeder, but they usually operate on a smaller scale. Reputable hobby breeders practice ethical, caring, quality standards, and take immense pride in their reputation and in their dogs.

Our third category is the breeder that you should avoid at all cost - the so-called "backyard breeder". These breeders are primarily interested in making money. They will promise you the world, tell you their standards are second to none, and that they are experienced, caring professionals; they will assure you that the dog they are ready to sell to you is healthy and comes from excellent lineage. Unfortunately, nothing could be further from the truth. You will most likely be the recipient of a dog who could be carrying a long line of genetic disorders, who has been poorly socialized, and who may have been taken from Momma Dog much too soon. Any certificates or registrations that were promised to you will happen to "get lost in the mail". You'll never see those papers because they never existed. The only thing that does exist is an unscrupulous, money-hungry thief whose only interest in dogs is the cash that lines their own pockets.

Now, you may ask, how is it that this author is so knowledgeable about backyard breeders? Because I, myself, fell victim to one of them. I often repeat this story as a lesson in what NOT to do when you're thinking about purchasing a dog. It's the story of Moxie, my Bernese Mountain Dog, who despite a sad puppy history, became the love of my life and an all-around, wonderful, long-time companion. I regret nothing in finding this amazing dog, except for my own short-sighted mistakes.

Some years ago, my younger, more naive self, became friends with an older gentleman who resided in the same town as me. He was the proud owner of a huge, bear of a dog, the likes of which I had never seen. (This all took place prior to my becoming a professional dog trainer.) "Moose" was a lively, joyful dog who would spend hours walking on the beach with Frank, his owner. Frank would never tire of pointing out what a wonderful pet Moose was and would chat for hours about the amazing attributes of the Bernese Mountain Dog.

I made up my mind that my next dog would be a Berner. Did I ever think to ask Frank about Moose's history, health, or the name of his breeder? Of course not. I only knew that I wanted a dog just like Moose. Sadly, Frank passed away, and I never saw Moose again; I never forgot Frank...or Moose... either. When the time came for me to bring a new dog into my home, I knew it had to be a Berner, but where would I find one?

Those were the early days of the internet, so finding a breeder was limited to scanning the "Dogs, Cats, and Pets for Sale" ads in the Sunday newspaper. One day, an advertisement from a breeder in Southern Vermont appeared for Bernese Mountain Dogs. Vermont was a somewhat manageable drive from my home on the North Shore of Boston. I called the number listed and spoke extensively to the breeder (who seemed quite experienced and caring). I was thrilled to learn that she had a current litter available; there were only two dogs left, a male and a female, who were three months old and ready to go to a loving home. The price seemed reasonable, and I asked when I would be able to drive north to see the dogs.

How "coincidental" it was that the breeder happened to be driving south to deliver one of the pups to a potential buyer although neither had been specifically sold yet. Would I like to meet her halfway and have first choice? It would have to be a cash transaction if I wanted to purchase one of the pups. (Now, what could possibly go wrong here?)

We arranged to meet at the parking lot of a fast food restaurant where she was waiting at the appointed time and place, and I immediately fell in love with the female pup. Smothered with puppy kisses and covered with black doggy fur, there was no doubt that I had found MY Berner! The breeder said that since she was not sure if I would want either of the dogs, she did not bring the health certificates or AKC registration information, but she assured me that she had everything in order and would mail them to me as soon as she returned home. You can probably guess the rest of the story.

Despite many phone calls, I received no further response from the breeder. There was no proof of any health-related tests. No certifications, no information on lineage. No answers to my questions. Nothing.

Moxie, fortunately, turned out to be a beautiful, sweet dog - one of the best dogs I have had the pleasure of owning. She was everything I anticipated. What I didn't anticipate was the veterinary expenses. During her lifetime, she suffered from hip dysplasia, elbow dysplasia, hyperthyroidism, food allergies, skin, and eye and ear issues. She needed several costly surgeries; her visits to the vet were sometimes on a weekly basis. She lived to be eleven years old, certainly beating the odds, considering all of her health problems. She was thoroughly pampered and greatly loved, and she left me with fond memories...and an empty wallet.

In retrospect, I only ask that you don't make the same mistakes. Was it costly? Yes. Was there heartbreak? Most definitely. Although my "perfect" dog wasn't so perfect from a health or financial perspective, we loved each other in a most perfect way. I considered it a learning experience.

My advice: Beware of opportunistic, unethical backyard breeders. They still exist, more so now than ever before. Do your homework!

Questions to Ask a Breeder

Once you have narrowed down your choice of potential breeders, you've still got some work to do. Here's a checklist with suggestions of questions that you should ask a breeder, but we encourage you to add any concerns that will aid in your selection of both breeder and dog:

✔ Do you have puppies available? If not, is there a wait list?

✔ How often do you have a litter available?

✔ Are we able to choose a specific dog from a litter?

✔ Do the prices vary from one dog to another?

✔ When will I be able to take my dog home?

✔ How long have you been breeding dogs, and what experience do you have with Bernese Mountain Dogs?

✔ What health testing and certifications do you provide?

✔ What initial vaccinations, de-worming, and other treatments will our dog have before we take him home?

✔ Do your dogs have any history of genetic disorders?

✔ How have your dogs been socialized?

✔ Are we able to visit your facility?

✔ Can we bring family members and other pets to meet our dog?

✔ Will we be able to meet the parents of our dog?

✔ What guarantees do you offer?

✔ If there are any unforeseen circumstances, including those relating to our dog's health or if our dog needs to be returned for any reason, will you take our dog back and refund our payment?

✔ Would a refund be in full or pro-rated?

✔ Do your dogs have certifications, and are they eligible for AKC registration?

✔ Do you have a breeding program?

✔ Do you have any requirements or provisions if we decide to show our dog in conformation?

✔ Do you require a spay or neuter contract?

✔ Can you provide us with referrals of people who have purchased a dog from you, and may we contact them?

Photo Courtesy of Brandy Vorwaller

✔ After purchase, will we be able to contact you with any questions we might have about our dog?

✔ Will it be necessary to sign a contract, and are we able to have our attorney view it and make any changes if needed?

✔ Do you require me to own my own home, or do I need written permission from my landlord?

✔ What questions would you like to ask about my household members and me?

There are certainly a lot of questions to ask, but a reputable breeder will most assuredly be amenable to offer answers.

It works both ways when it comes to breeders asking questions of buyers as well. An experienced and reputable breeder will want to ascertain that their dogs are going to homes where they will be well-cared for and loved. For this reason, be forthcoming as to what you can offer this potential new member of your family.

Questions a Breeder Might Ask a Prospective Buyer

- Why do you want a Bernese Mountain Dog?
- Have you had any experience with this breed?
- Are you familiar with potential Bernese health issues?
- Have you owned a dog before?
- Do you have other pets at home?
- Who are the members of your household, and what are their ages?
- Who will be the primary caregiver for the dog?
- Is your home large enough to accommodate a dog the size of a fully-grown Bernese?
- Do you own your own home, or do you have permission from a landlord to own a dog?
- If you live in a condo, are there any size/weight/breed restrictions set by the association or on your condo documents?
- Do you have the financial means to care for a dog and to cover any unexpected expenses?
- Do you have a veterinarian?

- Will you be spaying/neutering the dog?
- Will you microchip the dog?
- Are you planning to breed the dog?
- Is there a caregiver at home most of the time or, if not, will you arrange for a pet sitter or doggy day-care facility?
- Do you have a fenced yard and/or are you able to exercise the dog regularly?
- Will you be taking the dog for professional training?
- Do you plan to show the dog in conformation, or will it be a family pet?

Please don't be put off by questions that a breeder may ask; give honest answers and understand that a responsible breeder will only want the best for his or her dogs.

Breeder Contracts

Every Bernese Mountain Dog breeder will have differing opinions about whether or not a contract with a dog buyer should be required and what will be included in that contract. It will often depend upon whether you are purchasing a dog as a pet for your household or if you plan to show the dog professionally. Contracts are for the protection of all - the breeder, the buyer, and the dog. In general, a contract will address points such as owner and breeder responsibilities, payment terms, documents to be supplied to the buyer at the time of purchase, health tests, certifications, guarantees, and refunds. There may be special provisions for requiring spay/neutering, breeding, medical expenses, and legal fees, should a discrepancy arise. Every state has requirements regarding the sale of dogs. It's always wise to consult with an attorney before penning your signature to any contract.

CHAPTER 5
Chatting with a Reputable Bernese Mountain Dog Breeder

Interview with Bernese Mountain Dog Breeder, Jordan Tong

We spoke with Jordan Tong, a breeder of Bernese Mountain Dogs, to get his perspective on what people should know when thinking about purchasing a Berner.

Tong's Bad and Boujee, bred by Jordan Tong.
Owner: Karen Barnett

AB: How did you first become interested in becoming a breeder?

JT:I got my first Berner around 2013-2014; not specifically to breed but because that was the dog I wanted. I was in college, did quite a bit of research, and I also have a degree in Animal Science. Breeders of Berners are a small community, but now with the internet and social media, it makes researching so much easier. I found a dog online who was a very good representation of the breed; I purchased her with full breeder rights and then decided to purchase one more.

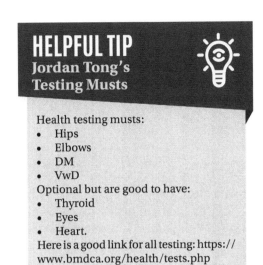

HELPFUL TIP
Jordan Tong's Testing Musts

Health testing musts:
- Hips
- Elbows
- DM
- VwD

Optional but are good to have:
- Thyroid
- Eyes
- Heart.

Here is a good link for all testing: https://www.bmdca.org/health/tests.php

After three years, I had one male and two females. I was not involved in the (dog) show world, but I did try to find dogs that would do well in conformation rings. I also raise birds - ducks, geese, chickens, and have numerous champions, so I already had some knowledge as to how to find a good dog. My grandmother raised Toy Fox Terriers for almost forty years, so we basically knew what to look for and how to get there. I was fortunate with my first Berner. She was a great dog.

AB: Is breeding Berners your only business?

JT: I actually manage a poultry layer operation with a couple million birds, but I don't consider breeding Berners as my hobby. It's more of a lifestyle. I would consider myself a "preservation breeder" because I'm conserving and preserving future traits that are desired. That's always the goal of a good breeder. You're selecting traits that are always going to be better in the next generation. I think people with children can relate to that - you're hoping that your kids will do better than you've done.

I don't breed as a full-time job or for my only income, but I breed wanting the next generation to be better when everything aligns. Right now, I have seven dogs, and there is a life cycle to consider. If you have dogs, you have to wait until they're two years old before breeding them. Plus, you always need a two-year gap in between the dogs.

AB: If someone has never had a Bernese Mountain Dog before, what would be the most important things that they should know about the breed in general?

JT: I would make the longevity issue very clear because people need to understand that. Eight years is a good life span for a Berner. I know someone who has a Berner who is fourteen, but I personally lost one at five years old. First and foremost, people need to know that Berners don't live as long as some breeds. You'll tend to have a dog with health problems if you don't do your research.

People should also know that they need to focus on grooming. If you don't like to brush or groom, and you don't like black fur tumbleweeds around your living room, don't get a Berner. My advice is to get a grooming table and an inexpensive blower, take your dog out, brush him out, blow him out once a week, and you'll be fine.

Another point, and I will use a Labrador Retriever as an example, is that this breed isn't like a Lab. A Lab wants to work. He wants to hunt. A Berner is in between a big dog and a little dog. They want to cuddle with you. They want to work for about twenty or thirty minutes, and then they're done. They're big babies.

AB: Do you check references or do any research on the people who are interested in purchasing one of your dogs?

JT: It doesn't matter to me if someone is purchasing for a companion pet or for show. I am interested in producing healthy, good dogs. I stay in contact with the people who have my dogs. You should be in communication with the breeder. If someone calls me, I will always try to answer any questions that they may have or point them in the right direction. When someone gets in touch with me to purchase a dog, I will ask how they found my contact information. I will never sell a dog without speaking with a prospective owner at length. I want to get to know them, and I want them to get to know me. That's important. About ninety-five percent of people are looking for a companion dog. I will ask whether they have any other dogs and whether they have ever owned a Bernese.

AB: If someone is just starting out and looking for a breeder, what advice would you give them?

JT: The simple answer for someone who is looking for a basic breeder would be to find one online. That's how most of them are found these days. Most of my dogs are actually sold by referral, but the most important thing a buyer needs is the dog's health information. Do not be afraid to ask for that paperwork. If the breeder doesn't have that information, or if you just have a bad feeling, then pass. This is such an important question. Ask to see the dog's pedigree.

I would also suggest that you contact your local kennel club or your local Bernese Mountain Dog Club. Every state has one, and they are such valuable resources to start with. Berner Garde is another excellent source. Most breeders will have no problem in helping you to find a dog or add you to a waiting list.

*However, I would tell people, if you're looking for a Berner, the most import-
ant thing to look for is their health information. Just be sure the dog has had
their hips and elbows tested. If a dog is structurally better, you're not going
to have those issues. That way you'll at least have predictability. We test for a
reason and that's to prevent problems. Again, the Bernese Mountain Dog Club
of America is an excellent resource for anyone interested in getting a Berner.
The people there have such great knowledge, and they've been doing it for a
long time. I would also tell anybody to go to a dog show and just talk to the
Berner people. They're always happy to talk about their dogs, and it's another
great resource.*

AB: Thank you, Jordan!

If you'd like to get in touch with Jordan, his contact information is:
Jordan Tong,
Marion, Ohio
740-361-7932
Email: jordanleetong@gmail.com

CHAPTER 6
Choosing the Perfect Pup

Take a moment to think about who you are. What does that have to do with choosing the right dog? Only everything. Are you more of the introverted type who is happiest sitting on the sofa with a cup of herbal tea and a good book? Are you an extrovert who never misses the opportunity to invite the neighbors in for an impromptu gathering? Would you rather go for a solitary hike in the woods, or would you prefer to spend the day on the beach with thirty of your nearest and dearest friends? Are you home alone most of the day, working remotely in your upstairs office, or do you treasure the sounds of small children running about, enveloping you in a constant stream of "Mommy, Daddy, I need..." fill in the blanks.

Photo Courtesy of Lauren Schmidt

Photo Courtesy
of Donna Murawski

Matching Personalities

"Bernese Mt. Dogs are great dogs, but one has to understand that the description of the breed character and temperament does not describe every Berner. In each litter there are dogs that are more outgoing, some that are a little more shy, and those that just sit and take the world in. One needs to match the right family with the right puppy so that the needs of both the puppy and the puppy owners are met."

SANDY NOVOCIN
Santera Kennel

*Photo Courtesy
of Gail Ruehorn*

The laid-back dog parent might do best with a laid-back dog - an older, more couch-potato-ish canine who only necessitates a few long, leisurely walks a day, and the occasional snuggle and belly rub. Would he enjoy a household of noise, a parade of neighborhood kids running through the kitchen, or dinnertime chaos? Possibly. But it may not be the best situation for an older, more reserved Berner.

On the other hand, a rambunctious pup may be delighted to have lots of energetic human or doggy friends join him for a romp in the yard. A more active family may be a match made in Heaven for this type of dog. Be open to all possibilities, but consider your lifestyle, your needs, and the type of dog with whom you'll be best suited. Happiness is sure to follow.

Male or Female?

Ask yourself if you have a personal preference. Have you owned dogs previously? If so, were you more partial to males or females? Every dog has unique characteristics, so it may boil down to the sex with which you are most comfortable. If you've always had female dogs, you may lean in that direction. Males are sometimes thought to be more aggressive, dominant, and territorial, but females are usually seen as more docile. Another factor that some owners consider is having to deal with a female dog when she goes into heat: attracting male dogs, bloody discharge, and possible aggression issues during this time of their reproductive cycle. Unless you're planning to breed, spaying early is highly recommended.

Most trainers, breeders, and veterinarians will suggest that if you already have a dog at home, it's preferable that the new addition be the opposite sex. Either gender may exhibit the occasional odd behavior, but early training will alleviate potential problems. Stereotypes are just that, and you can't lump all males or all females into one category. I've personally owned both males and females, and I usually opt for the girls. Ask me why, and I will honestly tell you that I have no idea!

FUN FACT
Luna the Berner

Luna is an Instagram-famous Bernese Mountain Dog living in Norway. As of 2020, she and her owner have amassed over 100,000 followers on Instagram. Luna was born on May 7, 2015, and delights her fans with photos of her scenic hiking adventures in Scandinavian forests and snapshots of her life at home. You can follow Luna's adventures on Instagram under the user name @ luna.the.berner.

Photo Courtesy
of Mykal Storey

Let Your Breeder be a "Match-Maker"

If you're purchasing Mr. or Ms. Puppy from a breeder, they will be able to give you some guidance on the specific characteristics of their dogs. Let them know if you have a preference or have a certain temperament to which you're partial. Your breeder will be familiar with his dogs' personalities and will be able to help with your selection. Want a more laid-back lad? The big guy snoozing in the sun may be just the right fit. Looking for Miss High Energy to accompany you on your daily hikes? Your breeder can make a recommendation. If you're able to meet the puppy's parents, you may be able to assess some of their traits. Is Doggy Daddy a lovable face licker

Photo Courtesy of Jess & Braeden Stoner

and a snuggler? Is Doggy Momma a bit more reserved and nurturing? Still, no guarantees either sex will grow up to be just like mom or dad. Every dog is special for his or her uniqueness. Male or female, you'll find the right dog, or more likely, the right dog will find you!

CHAPTER 7

Preparing for Your New Arrival

"Berners can be happy in many different surroundings. What they need most is to be around their family. They are very social and crave their owner's attention. They also bond quickly and are very loyal. A family is where they thrive as they are great with children and as I have personally discovered, they are excellent with special needs children and adults. They are also playful and like to 'help out' as much as possible."

MELINDA SUTTON
Beth's Bernies

Photo Courtesy
of Linda Helms

Choosing a Veterinarian

Your dog's veterinarian will be one of the most important people in your dog's life - the person who will be providing the professional health care your dog requires over the course of his lifetime. We'll sum up our best advice to you in two words: Choose wisely.

For those soon-to-be Berner parents with other pets already in the household, you're probably familiar with a veterinarian with whom you have an on-going relationship. If you are comfortable with their practice, then you might want to continue to bring your new family member there. However, ask your vet how experienced they are with the Bernese Mountain Dog breed. Berners, unfortunately, tend to have more health issues than other breeds. Some problems are genetic. If your vet knows to look for problems before they become advanced, it will certainly be to your dog's advantage.

If you don't already have a veterinary practice in mind, where should you begin?

A referral from other Berner owners would be a good place to start. Ask questions. Are they happy with the care their vet provides? Why have they chosen that particular practice? Why do they like their vet? This may seem like a basic question, but their answers won't always relate to what you consider most important. Be sure of your own priorities. As mentioned previously, my Bernese, Moxie, was a frequent guest at our vet's office so choosing the right veterinarian was a major decision.

While many dogs tuck their tails between their legs, panic at the sight of the waiting room, and can't wait to make a hasty exit, Moxie adored her visits to the veterinarian. There were so many visits, in fact, that if we had to make a long drive to get to the vet's office, the mileage on my car would have put me thousands of miles over my lease agreement. So, think about how far you're willing to travel. If location is important to you, no matter how wonderful your friend's vet is, you may want to reconsider. One concern I always had was fairly basic: In case of emergency, how fast can I receive care for my dog? In more rural areas, there may be no choice, but I like the reassurance of having a vet nearby.

What size practice would be best? Some people prefer a smaller office where your vet will be familiar with you and your dog. This has definite advantages. BUT...there are drawbacks as well. A smaller practice will likely have limited hours and fewer vets available, requiring you to wait days or even weeks to schedule an appointment. Of course, most vets will set aside time for urgent care, but it's something to think about.

Do you favor a more organic or holistic approach to pet care? What about alternative medical care? The veterinary practice you choose should be willing to work with you when it comes to your preferences.

Before you decide on a practice, make an appointment, and visit their facility. Is it clean? First impressions are important. (Keep in mind that all sorts of unexpected problems arise when it comes to animals in waiting rooms, so a less-than-desirable odor may greet you upon your arrival. It happens.) Pay attention to the overall atmosphere and attitude.

Photo Courtesy
of Lynn McLaughlin

Observations and Questions to Ask When Considering a Potential Veterinary Practice

- Is the staff friendly, caring, and happy to answer questions?
- Will they provide you with a schedule for upcoming appointments for check-ups, vaccinations, or spay/neuter information?
- What about charges for office visits and procedures?
- Do they accept pet insurance, and are they in the network you may be choosing?
- How long is the typical wait for an appointment, and what is their policy on emergency visits?
- What are their hours of operation? If you're on a tight work schedule, this could be one of the deciding factors. If they close at 5:00 p.m., Monday through Friday with no weekend hours, you might want to rule out this practice.
- What are their professional certifications, how long have you been in business, and do you have specialists in your practice; do you refer patients elsewhere, if needed?
- Do they have lab and surgical facilities on site?
- What about care of senior dogs? Although no one wants to think about it ahead of time, what is their philosophy and treatment regarding euthanasia?
- When making a routine appointment, are you able to choose a vet whom you prefer to see?

Are there certified veterinary technicians on site? (Often a technician can see a patient for a simple procedure, eliminating your having to wait a lengthy period of time to see a veterinarian. It may also be less costly.)

Finally, ask what forms of payment they accept. It's an important question. Too many pet owners have had to make emergency trips to the bank for cash if a practice only accepts a certain credit card...the one that you may not have...and many don't accept personal checks. It never hurts to find out in advance.

FUN FACT
Swiss Cheese Dogs

Bernese Mountain Dogs hail from Switzerland, where they originally worked as farm dogs. One of their tasks was often to act as delivery dogs. The carts that they pulled frequently carried milk and cheese, so the dogs were popularly nicknamed "Cheese Dogs.

Before Your Dog Comes Home

The big day is almost here! You're all set to welcome your Bernese into your home. Whether you've decided upon a puppy, a "teenager", or a senior dog, there are still some items that need to be checked off your to-do list. You, and perhaps your whole family, will be embarking upon a new journey. Is everyone ready? Supplies must be purchased, but first, there's that all-important home safety inspection.

Your dog sees things from a different angle than everyone else. You don't remember dropping that thumb tack a few months ago - you know, the one that got away and rolled under the sofa when you were hanging the bulletin board? However, from his vantage point, your new dog could find it, decide it's just a tasty morsel, and you've got a serious problem along with a trip to the vet.

This is the perfect time to do a thorough house cleaning. Actually, it's an essential time. Expect the unexpected when your dog arrives, and prepare everyone for things to be, shall we say, unsettled? At least for a while.

Photo Courtesy of Amy Wylan

Potential Dangers in the Home

"I stress to avoid letting your puppy jump on and off beds, couches, cars etc. Their growth plates don't close until around twelve months of age so keeping them from pounding on them is ideal."

STACY SLADE
Sevens Bernese Mountain Dogs

Whether your new arrival is a young pup or an older dog, there may be sights and scents that your dog has never seen. Berners are an intelligent, curious breed, and they'll want to smell and taste everything. Trouble will find them unless they are closely monitored. Keep your dog in sight at all times if he's roaming the house, and never underestimate his potential to get into something he shouldn't. The number of possible hazards is unlimited and include many items that you may never even consider. Make your new pet's safety your first priority! Let's take a walk through your home and see things through a dog's eyes.

Potential hazards include:

Kitchen

Under counter cabinets. A baby lock on all cabinet doors will ensure that your dog won't be able to access areas containing household chemicals, detergents, steel wool pads, string, and cleaning agents. Garbage cans, food and sharp knives left on counters, batteries, tobacco products, insect repellants, and plant fertilizers are all doggy dangers.

Living Room/Dining Room/Office:

Carpet fringes, window treatments and pull strings, candles, paper clips, elastic bands, electrical cords, any small items that could cause a choking hazard if swallowed. A puppy should never be allowed on a balcony, porch, or deck if there is even the slightest chance that he may fall under or wedge himself between a railing. Be especially careful at holiday time. Christmas ornaments, wrapping material, pine needles, and water in your tree stand can be extremely hazardous to your dog.

Family Room

Children's toys, puzzle pieces, phone cords and chargers, open windows and doors, fireplaces.

Bathrooms and Laundry

Toilet lids should be kept closed at all times, especially if cleaning agents are used. Personal hygiene products, razors, soap, toothpaste, medications, laundry detergents, dryer sheets.

Bedroom and Closets

Hair clips and accessories, wearing apparel (shoes, socks, and underwear are favorites for dogs to chew), medications left on a bedside table, mothballs and air fresheners, essential oils.

Other Safety Concerns

"Berners will eat anything and everything. Train yourself not to leave anything on the ground that they can eat. They are also notorious counter surfers, so be aware of what you leave in reach on the counters as well."

GIGI RAYMOND
Rhapsody BMDS

Additionally, there are many other items, both inside and outside of the home, which need special attention to keep your dog safe:

Crates

They're supposed to keep your dog safe and secure, right? Not always. If you've got a dog who's an escape artist, he could wedge his head, neck, paw, or leg between the door and the sides of the crate. Another BIG word of caution: Never, ever keep your dog's collar on him while he is in the crate. Imagine if you were gone for any length of time. In a concerted effort to free himself from that "safe and secure", newfangled contraption that he wasn't happy about being in, he managed to somehow get himself stuck. Dog collars + crates are an accident waiting to happen. It could be a matter of life and death, so be sure that it would be impossible for your sweet Berner to hurt himself.

Toys

Puppies, like young children, are fond of finding small objects to put in their mouths. Your new Berner is like a danger magnet - attracted to anything and everything that they shouldn't be. Keep plenty of "safe" toys on hand for your furry kid. Notice the word "safe" is in quotations? Even though a toy may be made specifically for dogs, there's no guarantee that it will be safe. Although they need toys and fun items to keep them physically and

Photo Courtesy
of Kimberley Rice

mentally active, a doggy toy can also be a hazard. Many of those cute, plush animals have squeakers in them, and yes, dogs love them. Every canine I've ever had the pleasure of sharing my home with has, within a matter of minutes, worked diligently to remove said squeaker. Caution! If your dog starts barking like Willie Whistle, it means he's eaten the squeaker.

The fleecy material on a soft toy can also be ingested by a curious pup. Too many vets have seen X-rays that reveal everything from fluffy teddy bears to mangled plastic chew toys. Simple household items can also pose a problem. Socks, underwear, buttons from clothing, wrist watches, shoe heels, parts of children's games or puzzle pieces, pillows and blankets, pens, rawhide bones (which, we will note here, should never be given to a dog), plastic dog food and water bowls - all can pose a hazard for your dog. Be ever vigilant, be watchful, and as you would with a child, know where your Berner is at all times; know what he's doing.

Foods

We've all regretfully fallen victim to those big, mournful doggy eyes - the ones that lovingly stare at you when you're chomping down on a ham and cheese sandwich or a bag of Cheese Doodles. For the health of your dog, and for your own sanity, DO NOT be tempted to feed your dog from the dinner table. If you do, you'll be creating a monster; a little beggar who will relentlessly be at your side waiting for table scraps.

Now, raise your hand if you can honestly say you've never fed a dog "people food". My hand is raised. Guilty as charged, your honor. So, if giving your dog a bit of your burger or a tidbit of turkey happens to be in your future, be aware that there are some human foods that your dog should absolutely never consume. Those foods include tomatoes, avocado, citrus fruits, onions, garlic, chocolate, raisins, grapes, nuts, caffeine, bread dough, coconuts, chewing gum (and other items containing xylitol), and alcohol. These substances are POISON to your dog. Just as some people are allergic to certain foods, dogs can also have allergic reactions. My dog has a severe pork allergy, so pork and pork by-products are banned from her diet. Poor little girl will never know the pleasure to be had from a crispy slice of bacon. Sorry, pup!

Indoor Plants

Those of us who possess a green thumb and a desire to bring a little bit of Mother Nature indoors are likely to have plants in the home. We love them. They're good for our household environment, fill up empty corners, and provide us with lovely, purified air. They make us happy. With your new dog arriving any day now, you'll need to wave goodbye to your precious philodendron and your beautiful, blooming begonia. Many plants are toxic to pets. The plants which aren't poisonous can still cause a major problem and an expensive veterinary visit. Think diarrhea, vomiting, lethargy - among other issues. In addition to the begonia and philodendron, other highly poisonous plants include jades, dracaenas, poinsettias, scheffleras, sansevierias, aloe, and calla lilies. Needless to say, you'll also have to wave good-bye to any spike-y cactus plants.

Even if your dog has not eaten any actual parts of the plant, pups love to dig in dirt, and what's that substance that keeps your plant alive? Correct! Dirt! Some dogs find the soil itself a tasty treat, while others just enjoy scattering the soil everywhere. Have you fertilized your plants? Sprayed them for those nasty mealy bugs or aphids? A dog who consumes dirt is headed for potential trouble. It may be in the form of a major clean up for you, or a digestive problem (or worse) for your dog. Donate, give away, or throw out those beloved plants. (Don't shoot the messenger.)

Outdoor Safety for Your Dog

Outdoor Plants

Your dog is susceptible to hazards outside the home as well as indoors. Plants such as holly, vinca, geraniums, carnations, daffodils, tulips, boxwood, foxglove, and lilies of the valley, among many others, are poisonous to your pet. Lawn treatment, applications of pesticides and fertilizers can cause health issues for dogs. If you're walking in public locales or along a neighbor's grassy sidewalk, keep in mind that the area may have been treated with chemicals that could be harmful to pets. We urge you to consult a pet poison-prevention center or research both indoor and outdoor plant sources which will list potentially toxic plants. (ASPCA.org is a valuable resource and maintains an extensive list.)

Is marijuana legal in your state? Ingesting the plant (or edible) can be lethal to our canine companions, depending upon the amount that a dog has consumed. Scientific research has yet to determine whether medically prescribed doses or oils from the hemp/marijuana plant, such as CBD, is beneficial in treating some illnesses in animals. We highly recommend that you consult with your veterinarian for more information and advice.

If you're fortunate enough to have a lovely yard in which your dog can run, play, and revel in the great outdoors, that's a big plus for everyone. Unfortunately, it doesn't mean that you can open the back door and say, "OK, go play. See you in a couple of hours!"

Sorry, but you're still responsible for keeping a watchful eye over your dog. Do you have a swimming pool? If so, does your dog have access to it?

Would you leave a child near a pool without careful supervision? Not all dogs can swim. Also, there are chemicals in the pool to which your Berner could have a reaction. If you have a pool and you're not outside, then your dog shouldn't be outside either.

Hot Weather, Cold Weather

By now, you know that Bernese Mountain Dogs are cold-weather animals. There's nothing more appealing to your big, furry dog than a winter snowstorm and a mound of fluffy white snow in which he can play. Although Berners tolerate wintry weather conditions better than most other breeds, use caution and don't allow your dog to be outside for extended periods of time.

Hot temperatures create definite issues for every dog, more so for BMDs. Keep your dog inside when the temps begin to creep up and keep them comfortable. Air-conditioned rooms, cool tile or concrete floors, and plenty of shade will help your Berner get through the dog days of summer. Schedule long walks for early mornings and after the sun goes down. Pay careful attention to streets, sidewalks, and driveways when the temperatures climb. Hot asphalt can quickly cause severe burns to your dog's paw pads. (If you're wearing flip flops or sandals, it's easy enough to slip your

Photo Courtesy of Lainey Mountjoy

feet out and test the ground. If it's too hot for your feet, it's too hot for your dog as well.)

Outside, supply plenty of fresh water, and watch for areas where your dog may dig a hole where he'll be cooler. My Berner decided that her favorite summer spot would be located underneath my huge, prized, rhododendron bushes. In the short amount of time that she was outside while I was planting petunias, she managed to excavate half-way to Australia. Needless to say, those formerly gorgeous pink rhododendrons were never quite the same.

Although your Berner will probably love her car rides, we can't stress enough the importance of NEVER LEAVING YOUR DOG IN A CAR IN WARM WEATHER. In some states, dog owners face hefty fines and criminal charges for leaving a dog unattended in a vehicle. It may be a balmy 70 degrees outside, but your Berner will quickly overheat. Dehydration, heat stroke. and ultimately, death can be the result of your poor decision to "just run into the store for a couple of things. She'll be fine in the car." No, she won't. Don't even think about it.

Critters and insects are yet another outdoor concern. Your dog has a thick coat, but that won't deter the bugs from biting her. Here's Part 2 - *Moxie, the Berner, Digs Up the Rhododendrons* - As she lay three feet below the surface of my yard, furthering her archeological escapades, a loud yelp was heard, presumably spelling trouble and another costly visit to the vet. My fears were confirmed as my precious dog's formerly cute face began to swell to the size of a giant watermelon, and her big brown eyes became swollen shut. Everybody in the car! Emergency! She was allergic to whatever random species of insect had stung her. Moxie somehow managed to survive yet another crisis. By this time, she was considered "a regular" at the veterinary clinic.

Besides your dog, what critters frequent your yard? Squirrels, rabbits, chipmunks, raccoons, fox and coyote, groundhogs, blue jays, and other furry, feathered friends? In addition to carrying diseases, possibly attacking your precious pup, and causing countless other concerns for humans and pets alike, it's just one more item on the list of reasons to not leave your dog outside alone.

Part 3 - *Moxie, the Wonder Dog, Strikes Again* - Late one afternoon, we were out in the yard with Moxie happily enjoying the cool summer breeze. Squeak! Squeak! Squeak! I turned to my husband and commented, "Oh, you must have left one of the dog's squeaky toys outside." Um...no, he didn't. We quickly followed the sound of the squeak, and noticed that in our dog's mouth was a baby skunk that our beautiful Bernese had thought resembled a chew toy. Pepe Le Pew managed to escape unharmed, and we were off to the groomers for an emergency de-skunking appointment. There's no end to the fun when there's a Berner around.

Preparing an Outdoor Area for Your Dog

Fencing and Dog Gates

A fenced yard is a lovely concept, but there are fences and then there are fences. A three or four-foot-high fence may be sufficient for keeping a small dog from leaving your property, but your Berner is not small - or won't be for long.

Photo Courtesy
of Autumn Wignall

Some breeders and rescues won't even consider allowing a dog to be placed in a home where there is not adequate fencing. A fenced-in area should not be looked upon as a substitute for giving quality time and attention to your dog; he needs human contact as well. If you've got the space and you're secure in the knowledge that your dog won't jump over the enclosure, that's great. However, there are a few things to keep in mind.

Many a calm homebody of a Berner has turned into an escape artist at the scent of a strange dog wandering in the vicinity, a friendly neighbor with a pocket full of dog treats, or a child who accidentally leaves a gate open. Berners are quite fond of digging and can easily excavate under a fence in a short amount of time. Also, sad to say, there are some unscrupulous people out there who wouldn't think twice about absconding with that big, beautiful dog with the wagging tail; a dog who would be delighted to follow a stranger into a car and then quietly disappear.

It's recommended that any fencing should be a minimum of five to six feet in height to prevent your fledgling Houdini from bolting over it and exploring the neighborhood. Invisible electronic fences are an alternative; however, they must be professionally installed. Your dog will also need to be trained so he knows where his boundaries are. Companies which install electronic dog fences will work with you and your dog to keep the potential shock factor to a minimum. However, it does take time, effort, and consistency. An invisible fence will NOT keep people from visiting your property and hanging out with your dog. Someone could always remove the dog's collar and lure him away from your property.

On a personal note, some years ago, after thoroughly weighing the pros and cons (and costs) of installing an electronic fence for my dog, I decided that it would be an excellent way to keep Moxie from wandering away from our yard. I contacted a very reputable company, had the perimeter of my yard dug, and the wires embedded in the ground. Warning flags were placed, and the dog was trained to know where she could and couldn't go. Everything went according to plan until Moxie decided that the shock discomfort just wasn't enough to keep her in the yard. She strayed, thoroughly enjoyed her mile-long walk, and was summarily "arrested" by our local animal control officer. I posted bail, the electronic fence lay dormant, and a "real" fence was installed.

CHAPTER 8
Supplies for Your Dog

"The best home for a Bernese is a home where they can live inside with their people and be part of the family. Berners love to be with their people. They don't do well as an outside dog only. They do however prefer moderately cool to cold weather as they have thick insulating coats."

STACY SLADE
Sevens Bernese Mountain Dogs

Photo Courtesy
of Travis Bannon

Crates

We'll offer information later in this book on the many reasons why you should crate train your dog. For now, because crates are so useful, we'll assume that you'll be using one. Keep in mind that size DOES matter, and the material that the crate is made of matters as well. There are two types of crates - metal and plastic. I recommend the metal for the simple reason that there is a chance, although minimal, that a dog can chew his way through the plastic variety. I've tried both kinds of crates, and I've always been fearful that even the smallest piece of chewed plastic could injure my dog. However, it's a matter of personal preference. Prices will vary greatly, so depending upon your budget, we'd advise you to shop around.

> ## FUN FACT
> ### Hannah the Bernese Mountain Dog
>
> Author and dog-lover Linda Petrie Bunch has written a collection of children's books about her Bernese Mountain Dog, Hannah. The collection consists of three books that are chock-full of color photographs of Hannah on her adventures. The author has owned and loved Bernese Mountain Dogs for many years and currently lives with three, Hannah, Lucy, and Dot, in Colorado.

Your pup's crate should be one that will be big enough to hold him no matter how big he gets. Some crates come with removable partitions that can be adjusted as your dog grows. This way, a young puppy has enough room to be quite comfortable but not enough room to find an out-of-the-way area in the crate to use as his bathroom spot. For a growing Bernese Mountain Dog, an extra-large size crate of approximately 48L x 30W x 33H inches is ideal.

Food

Your dog has become accustomed to whatever his breeder, foster home, or shelter has been feeding him. With so many changes about to occur in your dog's life, this is not the time to switch to a different brand. Speak with your pet's caregiver and ask what your dog has been eating as well as the amounts and frequency of his feedings. Not all dog food brands are readily available at all pet food establishments, so you should have a supply on hand for his arrival plus a few extra weeks. It's also a good idea to speak with your veterinarian to see if he or she will be recommending any changes in your dog's diet in the near future.

Food and Water Bowls

"Raised dog bowls are NOT a good idea. This encourages your dogs to eat faster, taking in more air and increasing your dog's chances of bloating. Eating from the ground like a dog in the wild would eat is always best."

AMY KESSLER
Lionheart Bernese

Again, personal preference. Metal, plastic, and ceramic bowls are easily available. My dog and cats use metal bowls for food and water. Ceramic bowls are heavier and more difficult for an active dog to tip over. If your taste runs to funky designer bowls, there are plenty of options in the ceramic category. Be sure they are lead-free, recommended for pets, and dishwasher safe. Plastic bowls make fun playthings, if your dog is so inclined and can be chewed by a very enthusiastic, energetic dog.

Metal bowls, usually made of stainless steel, can tip and move around easily; opt for those which have a rubber, non-slip ring on the bottom to keep it in place. Other types of bowls include the maze-like variety, made specifically for the dog who devours his food in lightning speed (It gets them to eat slower.), and silicone fold-up or thermos bowls (Excellent for bringing along on hikes.). The choice is yours.

Leashes and Harnesses

"Bernese must never know their own strength, they can pull 5 times their body weight, so from the time they are puppies, never walk them in a harness or on an extendable lead, always walk to heel on a proper lead or walk them off their leash."

MRS. PHILIPPA GREEN
Pasturegreen Bernese Mountain Dogs

Visit any pet store, and you're sure to be overwhelmed by the variety of equipment necessary to walk your dog. First, check your city or town's dog ordinances. There may be rules to follow. Some towns have implemented laws which make it illegal (Yes, that's correct!) to walk your dog on anything longer than a six-foot leash. A six-foot leash is the perfect length to

*Photo Courtesy
of Lauren Schmidt*

keep a dog under your control at all times. You'll have a choice of material - leather or nylon.

Most professional dog trainers will recommend the leather variety. These leashes will feel quite stiff at first, and they will be more expensive. However, they will "break in" quickly, will become very pliable, and will be easier on your hands than the nylon leashes. They'll last for many years if properly maintained. By properly maintained, we mean that you should keep it out of your dog's mouth. Dogs just love the taste of a good leather leash.

The leather leash I am currently using is 15+ years old and still in perfect condition. I have two additional leather leashes that I also use - one kept in each car, depending upon who is shuttling Puppy-face off to doggy day care or a walk in the park. All three leashes have outlasted several dogs.

You may be tempted by some of the specialty leashes. Oh, so you're a Red Sox fan and there's a nifty nylon leash with the Sox logo all over it. Or that pink rhinestone collar and leash set that would look stunning on Muffy. Don't trade cuteness for performance and your dog's safety. In all probability, you'll end up with blistered hands or a broken or frayed leash within a short amount of time. If that darling pink leash that's made for fashion and not functionality breaks while you're walking your dog (and chances are good that it will at some point), your dog's life could be at risk. Is that Red Sox logo worth taking the chance? Didn't think so.

Retractable leashes are not an option for you and your dog when he is a new arrival in your home. Until you are in total control when walking your pet, please don't even consider this type of leash. (Again, in many cities, these leashes are not allowed.) A retractable leash in the hands of an inexperienced dog owner or with a dog who is not at the stage where he can walk calmly by your immediate side, is dangerous. Wait until your dog is familiar with his commands, and you're thoroughly confident that the leash you're holding won't go whizzing out to its full potential of sixteen or twenty-five feet - and know that your dog won't end up in the path of an oncoming car. Another potential mishap: two dogs, both on retractable leashes, sniffing each other, pleasantly saying a doggy hello. The leashes become entangled. One dog decides to bolt. Have you ever seen the result of a "leash burn" on a dog owner's bare leg? It's not pretty.

Harnesses are great for smaller dogs, older dogs, and dogs with painful joints and mobility issues. A harness can also provide support for a dog who has trouble walking or standing; however, I have found that some dogs are less responsive to commands when a harness is used. Also, for those owners who suffer from a bad back or other physical limitations, it's sometimes easier to use a collar. If you're working with a dog trainer, he or she may have a recommendation as to which method will work best for you and your dog.

Collars and Identification Tags

Your choice of collar is, in most cases, a matter of personal preference, but with so many styles and materials to choose from, it could require a bit of trial and error before finding the right one. Leather collars are great and long-lasting but somewhat more expensive than nylon collars. Nylon collars are fine, and if you're looking for your dog to make a fashion statement, you're sure to find one that labels your pooch the star of the catwalk. (Sorry!)

Be certain that the collar is well-made, doesn't irritate or pinch your dog's neck or pull his fur, and fits well. Measure your dog's neck with a soft tape measure or length of string and add two inches to determine the appropriate size of collar. Collars should never fit too snugly. You should ideally be able to fit two finger widths between the collar and the dog's neck. It's important to check the collar periodically, both for durability and tightness. If your dog can back out of the collar, it's too loose and a definite safety hazard. Collars can stretch or shrink after getting wet so readjust for the proper fit. A mature, fully-grown dog can use the same collar for quite a while; however, they do need to be replaced occasionally due to wear and tear.

Identification tags are a MUST for your dog. If your dog is microchipped (something we highly recommend), it is still important to have an ID tag on the collar. Most pet stores have machines that will print a tag as soon as you purchase one. Should you put your dog's name on the tag? It's entirely up to you. I don't. My dog's tags simply state, "If found, please call phone number." In addition to the ID tag, the collar should also have an up-to-date rabies tag, your town's dog licensing number, and his microchip tag. That's a lot of metal jingling. A quieter solution is to place a strip of Velcro around all of the tags. No more noise!

Dog Beds

Have you heard the story of the dog who just adored sleeping in her owner's bed? Stella, the Bernese, had her favorite spot right between her human mom and dad. Mom and dad loved having their pup to snuggle up to and couldn't fathom the idea of not having their pet alongside every night. Stella's gentle, rhythmic snoring was so comforting to them. Stella considered the bed her territory. One day, Stella's human mom needed to change the bed linens. Stella was not happy and refused to budge from her comfy spot on the bed. Mom asked Stella to vacate. Dog refused to leave. Mom started raising her voice, dog decided to assert herself and defend "her" bed, and then Stella became aggressive and began growling. Mom was mortified.

Several days later, when her owners returned from shopping, they noticed a big wet spot where Stella had chosen to relieve herself on the bed, clearly marking her territory. Mom quickly contacted a dog behavioral specialist.

Moral of the story? Get your pet her own doggy bed, and do not allow your Bernese on your bed.

If you're crate training your dog, you can place her bed inside the crate. If and when you decide that a crate is no longer needed, your dog will still have her own bed. I keep my dog's bed on the floor NEXT to my own bed. Everyone's happy, she has her own space, and I am still close by. Many professional trainers can relate stories of the number of dogs they've seen with problems surrounding sleeping in their human's bed. It's an issue that can be avoided if you never allow the dog on the bed in the first place. Problem solved.

What type of bed should you buy? One that fits your dog, your budget, and your space requirements. Choices abound with gel beds, memory foam beds, cooling beds, pillow top beds, flat beds, bolster beds, snuggly fur beds, and beds for dogs with anxiety. There's a Murphy bed for your pup with a mattress that pulls down, a bed that fits into furniture, and there's even a futon dog bed. Orthopedic beds and elevated beds can be more comfortable for a senior dog with aching joints and musculoskeletal degeneration. There are waterproof beds for dogs with incontinence issues.

Consult with your dog's breeder or caregiver, and ask how your dog prefers to sleep - stretched out or curled up? If you're crate training, purchase a bed that will fit into the crate. You'll be replacing that bed many times throughout your dog's life. You need not limit your dog's bed to only one. My dog has 3 beds - one in the kitchen, one in the family room, and one in my bedroom. She loves to be in the same room as her human family, no matter what we're doing. She may as well be comfortable.

Coats and Paw Protection

Your cold-weather-loving dog will adore spending time outside on wintry days. Running through slush, chasing sleds down a hill, and watching you shovel load after load of a foot-high snowfall are all sources of immense joy to this heavy-coated breed. Bernese ancestors thrived in the snowy mountains of Switzerland, so pure enjoyment of cold, snowy weather is inherent. That doesn't mean, however, that your Berner won't benefit from some protection in the winter.

Streets and sidewalks are covered with various forms of ice-melt for our walking and driving safety. Those huge, furry BMD paws that we find utterly gorgeous can become cracked, raw, and injured when walking on treated surfaces. Salt, sand, and chemical solutions can create problems for Berner feet. Check your dog's paws whenever he's been outdoors in inclement weather and wash them to remove all traces of anything that can irritate. You'll also find dog boots available online and in stores (in extra-large sizes, of course). They will take some getting used to on the part of your dog; however, persistence and a healthy dose of patience here is key. I've never had a dog that was happy to wear them, but others say their pets don't mind.

Does your Bernese Mountain Dog need a coat for cold weather? Well, yes and no. Call upon your common sense to decide. A young Berner puppy won't have his thick, double coat yet, so some protection from the elements may be a good cautionary move on your part. However, an older dog with his double coat (of fur, that is, not the manufactured kind), usually won't appreciate another layer. A senior dog with limited mobility or arthritis may indeed benefit from a nice, fleecy, extra layer.

My dog always wears an all-weather coat when it's cool and wet outside. She's not a huge fan of going out in the rain, plus the coat saves me from having to dry her as much when she returns from a walk. When it comes to outdoor temperatures, Berners are more susceptible to heat problems than cold temperatures. If your dog lives in an area where hot temperatures and humidity are the norm, be sure to keep him cool. If you're hot, your BMD is probably twice as hot, so crank up the air conditioner, and let your dog chill out.

Toys

Every dog needs a supply of toys, both for physical and mental stimulation. Toys are fun, will keep your dog busy, and they can make for a wonderful bonding experience for your dog and his human family. Some dogs will chew contentedly on a favorite toy for hours. Others will enjoy a rowdy game of fetch or find the toy. It can be a good learning experience for your pooch. If your dog tends to become too aggressive with certain toys or games, stop immediately. Some dogs love a robust game of tug-of-war with a rope toy, but you'll need to exercise good judgment here if the dog shows any signs of hostility.

I'm not a fan of doggy tug-of-war unless the dog is already familiar with the command to drop his rope toy when you ask him to do so. For a dog, tug-of-war can become a battle to see who's Top Dog. Things can escalate quickly, and there's really no need for either of you to go down that road. Stick to something that's not quite as combative. You'll both end up winners.

Some dogs prefer soft, plushy toys while others love to chomp on rubber "Kong-type" chewy toys. Your main consideration when selecting playthings

*Photo Courtesy
of Michelle Divita*

should be, first and foremost, the safety of your pet. Anything that can be swallowed easily should be avoided, so keep a watchful eye and check periodically to see if that big, floppy, stuffed bunny is in the process of being devoured, limb by limb. A constant supply of dog toys can become costly, so if you're the do-it-yourself type, you can try making your own. Old athletic socks can be stuffed with an empty plastic water bottle and tied off for hours of noisy, crunchy fun for your pup.

A wonderful way to ease your teething puppy's mouth discomfort is to wet an old, thick sock and pop it in the freezer. Chewing on a frozen sock will be a welcome comfort and soothe your dog's sore gums. You can make dog toys by braiding old tee-shirts or strips of towels, and if your pup is old enough for treats, hide some tasty bits inside rubber dog toys. Most dogs love sinking their teeth into a tennis ball, and the squeaky ones made especially for canines are an extra doggy delight. Pet stores and on-line vendors offer an array of interactive toys for your pet, but your Berner will be just as happy to play a fun game of hide-the-Milk-Bone-under-a-red-plastic-cup. No matter how you decide to keep your dog occupied, practice safety first!

Poop Bags and Bag Holders

When the time comes to be out walking with your pet, every dog owner should be responsibly picking up after that dog. From a sanitation, health, and courtesy perspective, it's the right thing to do, each and every time. So please be considerate. You'll find plenty of options from pooper scoopers to designer, disposable, doggy bags. The bags run the gamut from the pricy bubblegum-scented pink plastic variety to bags personalized with your pet's name or your business logo.

Here's our bargain basement helpful hint: Unless you really need to impress someone with your customized doggy waste bags, head to the supermarket and pick up some boxes of bread/storage bags. Not the zipper kind, but the inexpensive ones with the plastic ties. My local market sells them for under two dollars for a box of seventy-five. The bags are lightweight, and you can keep several in your pocket on walks. (I always take a few extra bags in case of an emergency. It happens.)

Additionally, one item that I've found to be quite helpful is a small plastic waste-bag holder that attaches to the handle end of my dog's leash. They're available in pet stores and online for about five dollars, and they are an excellent investment. When you place the filled waste bag in the holder, it will free up both of your hands - one hand to hold the leash and one hand to pat your dog's head and tell him that he's a good boy.

Photo Courtesy
of Jess & Braeden Stoner

Treats

A pocketful of bite-sized goodies is essential to the happiness of your dog. Doggy treats will help keep your pup motivated to please you - in exchange for a bit of something yummy for his tummy. In addition to lots of praise when your canine companion responds in a positive manner to whatever you're asking him to do, a treat tells him that you're rewarding him for his good behavior. Small treats are best. If your dog loves a particular food, such as a piece of carrot or a bit of broccoli, take some on your walk, or keep them handy anytime you're working on training and commands. Don't overdo it or ruin his appetite with too many treats, and check with your vet to see if there is a specific brand that they recommend for your dog.

Odor Neutralizer

Keep a bottle (or two) in your home for those "Oh, no!" moments. Quality counts here, so forego inexpensive, no-name brands. Accidents can - and probably will - happen with your new Berner, and that applies to older dogs as well as young puppies. Odor neutralizers are formulated to remove canine urine and feces smells so your dog is not drawn back to the same spot where he's already gone. Do not use products that contain ammonia or vinegar because these scents can imitate the waste odors and can ultimately encourage your dog to repeat the offensive act in the same place. Be sure to test a small spot on furniture, floors, upholstery, and carpets first, and follow directions on the best procedure for use of the product. The quicker you can neutralize the odor, the more effective it will be.

Chewing Deterrents

"I think many families are surprised with teething, have many things for the puppy to chew, bully sticks, white knuckle bones, raw knuckle bones, antlers etc. They teethe and bite for a few months, it's normal. You can work with them on not biting you by replacing your hand with appropriate toys/chews. But constant chewing is important to relieve the pain of teething."

STACY SLADE
Sevens Bernese Mountain Dogs

A dog that's teething, anxious, or simply bored can resort to chewing anything within reach of his mouth. That item may include a sofa leg, your expensive Oriental rug, or a pair of new shoes. My tried-and-true go-to product is Grannick's Bitter Apple Spray, which many veterinarians recommend. Again, spot-test to be sure the cure won't be worse than the problem, but I've always been happy with the results. These products are non-toxic for your dog, odor-free, and MOST dogs hate the taste. Please note the word "MOST". You may have that one dog who is just not convinced that a bad taste is enough reason to stop devouring the special piece of woodwork that he's been working on so diligently. We'll address inappropriate chewing in Chapter 16 - our chapter on alleviating behavioral issues.

Grooming Supplies

"Probably one of the most important tools for a new Berner owner is to have a grooming rake. The undercoat of a Berner can make huge puffs of black hair all over your floor. The rake, which some breeds do not need, is an essential tool with a Berner owner."

SANDY NOVOCIN
Santera Kennel

Every Bernese Mountain Dog will have different grooming requirements. Chapter 19 will provide you with more details. There are some essential tools that you can purchase ahead of time since you'll want to get your Berner acclimated to a good grooming routine as early as possible. On their very concise website, the Bernese Mountain Dog Club of America recommends the following:

- Stainless steel pin brush
- Combs and Rakes – fine and medium
- Ear cleaner and cotton balls
- Dental care supplies
- Spray bottles
- Dog nail clipper or grinder
- Scissors
- Dog shampoo

Emergency Kit

On the ever-growing list of things you'll need to prepare for your new dog's arrival, it's a good idea to have an emergency kit specifically for your pet. How many times have we seen news reports of families who were reunited with their missing dog after tragic events or natural disasters? Or the worst-case scenario - the beloved pet is never found? There are a few ways to avoid possible catastrophe simply by planning ahead. Keep an up-to-date photo of your pet on your phone. (Well, that's easy enough to do. If you're like me, you've got more dog pictures on your phone than photos of your human family members.) If you're ever separated from your dog, you can make copies of the photos and distribute them around town or online.

Check with local hotels to see which ones take families with pets, as well as a list of phone numbers for those hotels. In the event of an emergency evacuation from your home, you won't have to spend precious hours making phone calls to see which locations will accept a dog. Many don't, and will not make exceptions. It's essential to have this information ahead of time. Pack a suitcase, bag or box with an extra leash and collar, water and food bowls, blanket, and first aid kit. Also include bottled water, toys, copies of your pet's health certificates and veterinarian's information, food, and any medications that your pet takes regularly. These items should be updated periodically to ensure that expiration dates and prescriptions are current. Keep a pet carrier/crate handy or whatever vehicle restraint you use for your dog. Make certain he is wearing his collar with all identification tags up to date. Then hope that you'll never need to use any of these items.

CHAPTER 9
Preparing to Bring Your New Berner Home

"Berners can be happy in many different surroundings. What they need most is to be around their family. They are very social and crave their owner's attention. They also bond quickly and are very loyal. A family is where they thrive as they are great with children and as I have personally discovered, they are excellent with special needs children and adults. They are also playful and like to 'help out' as much as possible."

MELINDA SUTTON
Beth's Bernies

Photo Courtesy of Dorothy Stephens

Location, Location, Location

Look around your home and try to picture where you'd like to "locate" your new dog. You wouldn't purchase a sofa and not know where it's going to fit, correct? Your Berner will need his own space and eventually, plenty of it. It's up to you to think about logistics.

It's ideal to have your dog nearby to see what he's doing but not so close that you're tripping over him while you're trying to get dinner ready. He'll need someplace to call his own, preferably to relax, take a nap, or sleep for the night. Whether you're using a crate or dog bed, try to locate it in a spot where he will be able to have some privacy, yet still know that his family is close by. If your budget allows for multiple crates and/or beds, all the better. Keeping one crate in a family room or kitchen and one in the bedroom for nighttime sleeping works well. Provide snuggly blankets and a few favorite toys for those times when he just wants to have his non-human friends nearby.

Where is your new arrival going to eat? Your Berner will soon be part of your family, and you and your household members are his pack. Eating with his pack is what comes naturally to your dog, so of course, he'll want to dine with you. Not at your dinner table, we hope, but somewhere in the vicinity. Place his food and water bowls in a low-traffic area but near enough for him to feel like he's with his family. An out of the way corner of the kitchen or dining room will give your dog the security of knowing he does, indeed, belong here.

Also, under the heading of logistics, is a toy box for your dog. I've got several in my home as a means of keeping things neat and tidy. (Good luck with that!) It really does help in keeping clutter to a minimum as well as saving your bare feet from the agony of stepping on a squeaky toy in the middle of the night. Doggy toy boxes are available in most pet supply stores as well as on the internet, and with low, soft sides, their contents are easily accessible to your dog.

Leashes should also be kept in a location that's handy. You'll be needing it several times a day, so if possible, keep one on a peg or hook close to the door you use when taking your dog for a walk. This is especially convenient when your dog must go outside to relieve himself at night. Trying to locate a leash is just not fun at 2:00 a.m.

Who's in Charge Here?

"The Bernese Mountain dog is definitely not a back yard dog. They thrive on human interaction. Be prepared to step over them as you cook your meals. They have a way of always laying down right at your heels! They are well suited for individual owners as well as families. The BMD does require some patience; they can be a bit stubborn in the learning process. It takes a lot of repetition and positive reinforcement but they are so worth it!"

DIANE CALDEMEYER REID
Faraway Farms Inc.

Photo Courtesy
of Derek Gaffney

A little planning will go a long, long way in preparing for your upcoming adventure with your Bernese Mountain Dog. It's important to determine ahead of time who's doing what. In a family situation, depending upon the age of the children in the household and their physical limitations, decide who will be in charge of walking, feeding, and picking up after the dog.

A young child should never be responsible for walking the dog, no matter how small the puppy or how docile an older dog appears. "Stuff" happens, so please don't take that chance. Respect for a dog's space and possessions, as well as those of a child, need to be enforced, along with limitations on playtime. A child or a dog can easily suffer injuries; for this reason, unsupervised play should never be allowed.

In any household where there's more than one dog parent, financial considerations should be discussed and agreed upon ahead of time. To put it bluntly, who is paying for what? Financial obligations can add up; supplies, food, veterinary expenses, doggy day care, training, must all be addressed. Be flexible and try your best to plan ahead for both unexpected emergencies and impulse purchases, but most importantly, be prepared.

Introducing Your New Berner to Other Pets in the Home

If your new Berner will be an only fur-child, this section may not seem as relevant for your planning dos and don'ts. However, if you already have a pet or pets in your household, this section will be an extremely useful tool in making the transition to adding another four-legged family member. You may already have a perfectly well-behaved dog or a lovely, cuddly cat, but what happens when you add another animal into the mix? Hopefully, nothing. Then again, who knows? Best to prepare ahead of time and allow for an amicable introduction. It will take a bit of forethought, but we can promise that it will be worth the effort.

Anyone who has more than one pet knows that jealousy can rear its ugly head at any given time. I presently have two cats and my dog, and Heaven forbid, I should make the mistake of sneaking Puppy-face a nibble of cheese without offering a smidgeon to her feline siblings. If I'm dog-sitting for my adorable Tibetan Terrier grand dog, the cats will spend the entire visit sulking until said pooch goes home. These critters rule their proverbial roost, and their daily routine, treats, feeding times, and entertainment is well established; in their minds, there is absolutely no need for modification. Or else.

Changes may seem minor to a human, but to a pet, it's a major adjustment that can have long term ramifications. The old recliner in the family room that was once Fluffy's favorite sleeping spot? It's about to be commandeered

Photo Courtesy
of Brian St.Onge

by some crazy canine cretin who just bolted through the front door and took over his chair! Who IS this, and why is he smelling up my sacred sanctuary?

There's never any guarantee your pets will become those lovable, best friends for life that we see on internet videos. Your cats could forever be disgusted by the mere presence of your Berner. Your current dog may barely acknowledge the existence of the newcomer. We always hope for the best, but sometimes mere tolerance for one another is perfectly acceptable.

Here are a few helpful hints when introducing your pets to one another. Animals have that keen ability to recognize a distinctive scent. Before your new dog arrives, bring an item into your home that's been with your new Berner - a toy, a towel, or a blanket. Let your established resident pets check it out so that they become familiar with the scent of the new kid on the block.

For peace to exist in the kingdom, it's especially important to introduce a new dog to an old dog on neutral turf - ideally a park or someplace away from your home, which your current dog does not consider "his" territory. Have both dogs leashed, and with the help of another person, allow them to sniff each other in a quiet, friendly, casual manner. Once they have established that neither dog is a threat to the other dog, bring them into the home, but keep the new dog in a separate area - one that's in a location where they can see each other and continue to get acquainted, without physical contact. They should both have their own beds, food and water bowls, and toys in their separate spaces.

Be sure to give each pet an equal amount of attention while keeping the atmosphere as calm and low-key as possible. A baby gate that's placed securely between rooms is ideal for keeping the dogs apart, yet within "getting-to-know-you" distance.

If there is a cat in the household, you will need to ensure her safety, whether your arriving Berner is an older dog or a puppy. Litter boxes, food and water bowls, and cat toys should be placed out of reach of the dog. Her "space" should be maintained, and she should in no way feel frightened of the dog. When the cat seems comfortable enough in the presence of the dog, keep the dog on a leash, and gradually allow them to check out one another at a closer distance. If you have the type of cat who is curious and agreeable to meeting the dog on closer terms, allow them to sniff each other and get acquainted while the dog is leashed. For the most part, they will establish their own boundaries. You will need some patience, as it could take a bit of time before they are accepting of one another.

My own dog and cats have never been the best of friends. If the dog invades their space, the cats will not hesitate to give her a good slap on the head, which is all it takes to send the pup scurrying for cover. They seem to have worked out a somewhat peaceful existence - at least until the next critter arrives.

Choosing the Perfect Name for Your Dog

Remembering the days before I brought Moxie home, I can honestly say that I spent more time trying to decide on the perfect name for her than I spent on naming my human kids. Research on "Great Names for Bernese Mountain Dogs" produced such gems as Bear, Max, Samson, Rocky, and Bernie. I found many big-boy dog names, but it seemed that big-girl names were in short supply. Suggestions like Lily, Chloe, Daisy, Bella, and Fifi evoked visions of a petite Yorkshire Terrier - not a large, not-so-dainty Bernese.

After days of anxiety over a fitting name, an elderly neighbor happened to stop by our front yard to say hello to my new pup who was zipping across the grass in a frenzy of unbridled energy. The dog stopped only long enough for a quick meet and greet, a sloppy kiss, and a treat; then she circled around to tear up some newly planted flowers. "Goodness, she is just full of moxie!" my neighbor commented. Moxie! That's it! My little girl finally had a name.

Photo Courtesy
of Aubrey Ross

If you're adopting an older dog or a dog that's been in foster care for a while, you may not have the opportunity to give it the name that you'd prefer. With so many new adjustments and changes, this is not the time to expect a dog to respond to a brand-new name. However, you may be able to come up with something similar that will be easy for your new pet to get used to. Bailey could become Hailey, Zeus could become Moose, or Charlie could become Harley.

If you're welcoming a young puppy into the household, it's easier to start fresh with a name that the whole family agrees upon. A rule of thumb in the dog-naming game is to keep the name short. One or two syllable names are best, since a longer name will likely become short-ened after a while anyway. Maximillian will doubtlessly become Max, and Penelope will become Penny. In case of an emergency, or if you need to get your dog to respond to you immediately, it's more important to call out a simple one or two-syllable name: "Casey! Come!" will be a much faster atten-tion-getter for your dog than, "Chrysanthemum! Come!"

No matter what you decide to call your dog, please don't use his name with anything that he will associate with negative behavior. For example, don't say, "Gus! You're a bad dog!" or "Gus! You dug up my marigolds! Shame on you!" Use his name for everything good. "Gus, good boy!" Offer him small treats and call him by name. "Here's a treat for Gus! You're the best dog!" It's amazing how quickly your dog will begin to respond to his new name when something tasty or a bit of praise is involved.

As a dog trainer, I would always offer this cautionary advice: Many dogs tend to "live up" to their names; Brutus might very well have some bully-ish tendencies just as Rambo and Fang might fulfill their name sakes. Cruella may have been fine for 101 Dalmatians, but somehow, it's just not a dog I'd picture as an adorable snuggle-bug. Whether it's in the name itself, or the connotation, I'd feel more comfortable having my sweet Moxie play in the park with a dog named Cupcake than a dog named Cujo!

CHAPTER 10

Welcoming Your Bernese Mountain Dog to His New Home

"It's important to remember when you bring your puppy home every single thing will be new to them. They will need reassurance, consistency and patience. But realize the routine you create from the beginning will be important as each time you change how you do things, it will set your puppy back in learning the routine (sleep in a crate, eat in the crate, route to potty, where to potty, etc.) you want them to learn and understand."

STACY SLADE
Sevens Bernese Mountain Dogs

Photo Courtesy
of Nick Timmerman

Photo Courtesy of Sheryl Carbone

The Ride Home

"Going home is such an exciting time! Make sure you puppy proof the area where they are going to be spending time. I always recommend crate training with a crate that incudes a divider to be used while the puppy grows. The crate should be in a quiet place so that the pup can rest when tired. Be careful of slick flooring and stairs with a young BMD. As they are growing they should not be jumping on and off furniture or in and out of cars. Give those hips and joints the best shot at developing properly! They are the foundation for a good long active life!"

DIANE CALDEMEYER REID
Faraway Farms Inc.

You can't wait to introduce your new dog to his forever home. We all have that picture-perfect arrival etched in our imaginations, with everyone oohing and aahing over the new member of the family. However, this scenario may be closer to reality: Your dog's just been (lovingly) scooped up and taken from his former home. He's wondering where he is, who you are, what's going on. He might be car sick, hungry, or just plain scared. You're probably anxious, too, and he will sense that. So, stay as calm as you can, offer him soothing words, maintain a quiet demeanor, and bring your dog home to a calm household. If you have young children, consider acquainting the dog with his new home when the kids are at school or at Grandma's for the day. Let him get accustomed to the unfamiliar surroundings on his own terms.

We all love that vision of the kids sitting by the Christmas tree, opening a beautiful gift-wrapped box of brand-new puppy. It's the Norman Rockwell syndrome. In actuality, the tree lights are flashing, the kids are screaming with delight, the relatives are scheduled to arrive for dinner in an hour, you're still in your pajamas, and Uncle Archie is already on his third Bloody Mary. Is this really the best time to introduce an apprehensive dog to the family?

Whether you'll be traveling across town or across the country, you should prepare for the trip home with your new dog. This is "Anything Can Happen

Photo Courtesy
of Lisa Gordon

Day"! While we hope that all will go smoothly, there are always a few "what ifs" that can occur even under the best of circumstances, so prepare for the unforeseen event. You'll need to bring your dog's new collar and leash, (be sure to put the collar on your dog before you begin the ride home), and check that he can't slip his head out of that collar. Bring paper towels, a toy, treats, bowls, food, and water for a long-distance trip, and if you're traveling in cold weather, bring a blanket. Don't feed the dog a big meal before the drive.

Give your dog a chance to relieve himself before getting into the car and make frequent stops if you're traveling far. However, if your new dog has not yet had his vaccinations, try to avoid any areas where dogs may have relieved themselves. Until he is up to date on his puppy shots and unless your breeder and/or veterinarian approves, keep him away from other unfamiliar dogs. If you can, take along a toy or blanket that has his mother's scent. It will comfort your new pup in Momma Dog's absence. If you are planning to use a car harness, this is the time to start; enlist an additional family member or friend who can sit nearby to provide some cuddles and reassuring words.

The First Night at Home

"Have the puppy in the room with you in a crate so when they whine to go out, you can take him out quickly. They want to be with their family. The first couple of days are difficult because they miss their siblings."

GIGI RAYMOND
Rhapsody BMDS

The ride home is over, so now you can give your Berner some time to check out his surroundings. Everything is strange to him. If he's a puppy, he may be away from Momma Dog and his litter mates for the first time. He needs reassurance that he's safe. Go slowly when introducing the dog to unfamiliar faces and places; a baby gate will work well for blocking off a room. This is all unfamiliar territory, so let your dog sniff to his heart's content, but don't let him wander too far.

If your new arrival is an older dog, the same rules apply. Put the neighborhood children on notice that visits to meet the dog will have to wait until he settles in a bit. Whether he has been in a shelter, with a breeder, or with a foster family, you might notice some quirks. The dog won't know what is expected of him, where he should go to relieve himself, or what is off limits. In the midst of all this confusion, a dog who is house trained might forget that he's supposed to wait to go outside. Give him time to adjust. Feed him, offer him water to drink, and take him out on his leash immediately to the

Photo Courtesy of Anna Snider

area that you'll want him to use as his permanent bathroom spot. When he goes, keep your voice upbeat, tell him he's the best dog in the world, (give a small treat), and show your approval for the good behavior.

Start a routine and practice consistency as soon as you can. Lots of praise, some treats, and a gentle voice will go a long way toward making the dog feel at home. Above all, don't yell. It will get you nowhere - except making a dog who is already frightened and confused even more so. If he relieves himself in a spot that's inappropriate, your tone of voice should be one of quiet disappointment, not anger. Your new dog does not yet know what he is supposed to do. It will be incumbent upon you to teach him.

However, when he DOES do something that's good, the praise should be abundant.

A calm, hearty "Good boy!" and a small treat will be much appreciated by your new pet. (Make sure to use the dog's name. He'll associate it with everything that's wonderful in his new world.)

Perhaps your dog is behaving in a totally admirable manner. He listens, he's relaxed, he responds to everything you ask, he's playful, and he's just all-around perfect. Shouldn't he be doing something inappropriate? Dog trainers often refer to this as the Honeymoon Phase. Berners are smart, sensitive beings, and your new dog is quietly observing. He's on his best behavior, but he's sizing up everyone and everything.

He's thinking, "Who is Alpha Dog? Who is Top Dog? Who is in charge? Who is the Commander in Chief around here? Who doles out the treats? Who feeds me, takes me out for walks, accompanies me on bathroom outings? Hmmm.... let's just chill for a bit and see who I'll need to listen to."

The Honeymoon Phase usually lasts for about two weeks, or until your dog comes to the realization that he is now comfortable in his new home; then, if he decides that you're not capable of assuming the role of Alpha Dog, by golly, he'll be delighted to take over that job...thank you very much! However, if you've made it clear in a gentle and concise way that you're not putting up with any shenanigans, he'll think otherwise. Be ready.

Introducing a Crate – Potty Training from Day One

We'd like to assume that you've made up your mind to crate train your dog. If not, house training may be the deciding factor. Whether you're a first-time dog parent or an experienced owner who's had dogs their entire life, you can expect to lose a little sleep the first night...week...month...when a new dog arrives. In addition to some canine snoring, you may be awake and listening for unfamiliar sounds that alert you to Mr. Dog's need to go out to relieve himself. Or he may be letting you know that he is lonely, uncomfortable, scared, or hungry.

Before you go to bed, think ahead. Your dog may not be able to wait very long to relieve himself, and you'd like to avoid any unnecessary stress - for you or the dog. Hang his collar and leash in a spot where you'll easily find them on your way out the door. It will be dark, so you'll need a flashlight. Whatever you're using to scoop his poop should be readily accessible as well, whether it's a pooper scooper or plastic baggies. Have your clothes, shoes, robe, whatever you need, close by. If your local meteorologist is calling for rain, snow, or ice, have the necessary weather gear handy.

Pay attention to the sounds and actions of your dog. He may whimper, spin in circles, bang on his crate, or bark. Successful bathroom training relies on both consistency and quick action on your part, so if you think your dog is trying to tell you that "it's time," take his word for it. He's gotta go.

Consistency also involves using the same door when you take the dog out, bringing him outside to the same spot every time, and using the same words when you refer to his potty ritual. My preferred words in the potty-training process are "go do peeps" and "go do poops". Three syllables. Keep it simple. The words you use are strictly your own choice. You could say

"Number one" or "Number two" if that's your preference, but don't change it up. Your dog will soon associate your words with his actions.

Your Berner must be taught to differentiate between daytime and nighttime potty training. When you take him out in the daytime, you can practice a more leisurely and casual approach. Bring him to the spot where he should go, use your preferred words, and then praise him for doing a good job, give him a treat, take him for a walk, hang out with him, or give him some quality play time. At night, however, he needs to know that it's all business. When it's his potty time, quickly put on his collar and leash, take him out, use your words, when he's done say, "good boy", and put him right back in the crate. Limit outside time to ten or fifteen minutes at most. No nonsense, no playing, no treats. Now everybody...go back to sleep!

How long can you expect your dog to wait in between bathroom breaks? Most veterinarians and trainers will advise you not to give your dog food or water before bedtime, and this is especially true for puppies. At a young age, bellies and bladders are small and can't hold much food and water. There's a simple theory for timing the distance between potty hours: A dog who is three months old should be taken out to relieve himself every three hours. A dog four months old or older should be able to wait approximately four hours. Gradually, extend the time by a half hour as the dog gets older, until he is able to sleep through the night.

A little trick that I have always taught my dogs during the daytime house training process is to ring a bell to go out. I attach a bell on a ribbon and tie it to the doorknob on the door used to take him out. Initially, I stand so that the bell is close to his nose, ring it myself, and say, "Do you want to go out to do peeps and poops? Ring the bell!" Dogs usually understand this maneuver fairly quickly. (Praise the dog, of course, when he gets the concept.) Positively reinforce this good behavior every time he needs to go out to relieve himself. The only drawback is that you'll need to train him to ring the bell ONLY when it's time to go potty. Otherwise, he'll figure out that he can ring the bell to go out anytime he feels like taking a romp through the yard to chase a squirrel or hang out with the neighbor's dog.

Crate Training Your Bernese Mountain Dog

Best Case Scenario: Your Berner loves his crate. It's his go-to place to sleep, to hang out, and to get away from the hustle and bustle of household activity. Worst Case Scenario: He hates his crate. He cries, whimpers, hides, or barks whenever it's time to go in. It's up to you to provide that quiet space that he calls his own and in which he can happily chill out. He needs to see his crate as a positive experience, so never send him to his crate as punishment.

Except for his nighttime sleep schedule, don't keep him crated for prolonged periods of time unless you're unable to be at home to watch him.

If your puppy is away from his mother and litter mates for the first time, he'll be scared. If you have something with their scent on it, let him snuggle up with that in his crate - a blanket, towel, or soft toy works well and may be just the comfort he needs in this unfamiliar environment. Let him relieve himself outside before he goes in the crate, so you'll at least know he's not crying because he needs to "go."

It helps to put some pee pads on the bottom of the crate just in case. It will make clean up easier if he does have an accident. Put his bed and/or some soft blankets in the crate as well and make it as comfortable for him as possible. Introduce your dog to the crate by leaving the door to it open and allow him to check it out by himself. He may decide on his own that it's a wonderful place to play, relax, or take a snooze.

During the day, you can give him treats in the crate and even put his food bowl in there with the door open. This lets him know that there's something good inside, and he'll look forward to being in there. (Water bowls will spill easily, so not a good idea.) Chewy dog toys to keep him busy are also fine to put in the crate for him although not at night. A rubber doggy bone stuffed with treats will keep him occupied in his crate for a while. When it's time for him to go into the crate, lead him in by pointing to the open door, using your words, and give lots of praise, encouragement, and a small treat for going in.

Be consistent, and above all, patient. Keep your voice upbeat, calm, and tell him he's the best dog ever! Eventually, you'll be able to trust him enough that he won't need the crate at all. Some dogs, however, love their crates, so it may actually become a permanent fixture in your home.

Congratulations! You've made it this far, and you're enjoying the role of being a pet parent to a Bernese Mountain Dog. Give yourself a huge pat on the back and give your dog a loving pat on the top of his big, furry head!

Photo Courtesy of Leslie Dalzell

CHAPTER 11
Doggy Manners

Now is the appropriate time to assess your dog's general behavior. Overall, it seems like he's doing well. Has he developed a few little idiosyncrasies lately that you've let slide in an attempt to be a kind-hearted dog parent? He's now feeling comfortable in his new home. He's got the pecking order figured out. He's fairly sure he knows who Alpha Dog is but wonders if there's a little wiggle room there. It may be that the Honeymoon Phase is just about over. Is he barking at the door? Play biting and nipping? Jumping up? Acting out just a wee bit? Welcome to Doggy Etiquette 101.

Photo Courtesy
of Brenda DeRenzo and Jamie Barton

Photo Courtesy of Andrée-Anne Frigon

The Importance of Training Your Berner

BMD's, in my experience, require positive reinforcement to train. They want to please and respond well to repetition. Once they figure out what you want they will repeat the positive outcome. It is very important to stay consistent in your training. Consistency and repetition are the key to your success!

DIANE CALDEMEYER REID

Faraway Farms Inc.

Human kids are taught the essentials of how to act respectfully in public, appropriate vs. inappropriate behavior, and basic good manners. We all try to raise our offspring to be kind, to know the difference between right and wrong, and to be respectful. Why should our dogs be any different? The simple answer is they shouldn't. It's your responsibility to teach your Berner to be sociable, respectful, and well-mannered. He won't learn those things by himself. Without your guidance, he will revert to his basic animal instincts. Owing to their intelligence, their willingness to learn, and their desire to

Photo Courtesy of Stacy Barkley

please their owners, Bernese Mountain Dogs are not considered difficult dogs to train.

My current dog came to me at the age of four months old, and I am convinced that she was born an old soul. Other than some simple commands, she never required any formal obedience training. If she is outside and off leash, she keeps us within her sight at all times, is content to hang out in the yard while we do our gardening or chat with neighbors, and at the age of eight, is an absolutely adorable homebody of a dog. Other dogs I've had have not been quite as mellow. One of my dogs, Murphy, was so, shall we say, precocious (and that's being very kind) that she was enrolled in dog obedience school immediately, and after many, many sessions, she finally earned the title of Star Pupil.

It was Murphy who inspired me to pursue a career as a dog trainer. She arrived at my home on day one as a feisty, high-energy pup - very assertive though lovable. She had that "hold my beer and watch this" attitude. It took patience, consistency, respect, and love on both our parts, but we eventually had a well-mannered, sociable dog, and I was an immensely proud owner. Murphy later became a therapy dog, with a penchant for making all who knew her smile. She visited hospitals, schools, and nursing homes; she brought joy wherever she went. Contrary to popular opinion and that old adage, you CAN - and should - teach an old dog new tricks. Those "tricks" don't come easily, however, and it will take some effort.

In the canine world, Mother Dog takes a no-nonsense approach to bringing up her offspring. If one of her pups is acting in a way that meets with her disapproval, she won't hesitate to growl at said miscreant in order to correct the errant behavior. As the new Mother Dog, you are the one raising your furry kid to know right from wrong; you are the one responsible for teaching all things appropriate and acceptable.

Let us note here that when we refer to "Mother Dog" or "Momma Dog", as it pertains to your Berner's training, if you're a male, you're still "Momma Dog". Please don't take it personally. In the dog world, male dogs tend to be less nurturing and authoritative when it comes to bringing up their offspring. It may be because as we domesticated dogs, we have, for the most part, eliminated the importance of the father dog in taking care of their young. Dogs are descended from wolves, and in the wild, alpha wolves, both mother and father, play an equal role in raising their pups. However, as our canine friends have evolved into family pets, the natural instincts, nurturing, and teaching roles have been relegated to mother dog. Momma Dog, Alpha Dog, call it what you will - you're the one who's in charge.

Positive Reinforcement – The Best Approach

"Never discipline a Berner with more than a stern voice. They are too soft hearted and do not require anything else. And even at that, make sure and give them plenty of loving and hugs after so they know you're not still mad at them."

Melinda Sutton
Beth's Bernies

Positive reinforcement is the key to training your Berner. Let your dog know that you're happy about something he's done well. Use his name in a cheerful manner when you're praising him. "You rang the bell to go out... you're a very good boy, Henry." A pat on the head or a treat, and your dog will be happy that you're happy. Conversely, if Henry has just chased the cat under the bed, there's no need to raise your voice. Adopting a quiet attitude of disappointment will let Henry know that you're not pleased with his behavior. "That's not a good thing to do." Don't use his name, no treats, no understanding comments. Your quiet voice will get the point across. Good or bad, keep the excitement to a minimum, but let the dog know whether you're approving of his actions or whether you feel he's made a poor choice. If you're a yeller, things will escalate quickly. In doggy language, he'll interpret your shouting as the equivalent to his barking.

Puppies have a short attention span and get bored easily, so don't drag things out. If you don't think he "gets it" and he continues to ignore you, a change of scenery will often help. Keep a collar and leash on him, and take the dog to a different room, provide a diversion, and take his mind off the offending behavior. Work on it another time when he's more responsive.

An older dog may need an even quieter approach. If your dog has been neglected, abused, or is shy, your disapproval may elicit a timid or scared response on his part. He may back away from you, frightened. Find a better word than NO, which might be a word he has heard a lot of in a previous home. Use a phrase like, "That doesn't make me happy." or "That's not a good thing to do."

If your dog committed a major felony, you could give him a brief time out. Don't continue it for long though because after a minute or two, he'll have no idea what he did that was wrong.

Consistency Counts

"Plan to take your puppy to a good puppy class and then continue with a basic obedience class. I cannot stress this enough. An untrained 85 -120 pound dog is NOT a joy. Even very experienced trainers take their dogs to classes for the socialization factor and learning to behave around other dogs and people."

BARB WALTENBERRY
Barberry BMD

Your Berner will be quick to understand what you're asking of him if you provide him with clear, simple techniques and words. Establishing a routine is especially important. You may tire of doing and saying the same things to him, but that's how he will learn best. In working with your dog, divide your sessions into short segments. You may have an hour of free time that you can devote to a training session, but to your dog, that hour will seem like a lifetime. He'll get bored and lose interest quickly. Five minutes of training several times a day, accompanied by encouragement, praise, and treats, will be much more effective. End all sessions on a positive note, and your dog will look forward to working with you.

Consistency also counts with family members in the same household. Be sure that everyone is using the same words and doing the same things. Everyone should be taking him to the same door to go outside to relieve himself, and household members should be using the same command for him to sit, stay, pee, poop, etc. If you don't want your dog to be begging at the dinner table, don't allow anyone to feed him table scraps. Also, he should never be allowed to jump on people at any time. Your ninety-pound Berner can easily injure a small child or an unsuspecting adult. It's all about good doggy manners.

ON THE BIG SCREEN
Good Boy!

Good Boy!, directed by John Hoffman, is a comedy film released in 2003 and based on the book *Dogs from Outer Space*, written by Zeke Richardson. The film follows a boy, Owen, who works as a dog walker so that he can show his parents he's ready to adopt a dog. Eventually, Owen's parents allow him to get a Border Terrier that he names Hubble. Owen soon learns that Hubble is actually from outer space and hopes to take over the world. Among the fluffy cast of characters in this family comedy is a Bernese Mountain Dog named Shep, voiced by Carl Reiner.

R-E-S-P-E-C-T

"BMD's are very treat motivated! Although that makes it easy in the beginning you need to be sure you are working with a trainer who will tell you when treats can slowly be phased out. A dog that is too treat dependent can become stubborn and refuse to obey unless you have a tasty reward for them."

ROBIN WORTS
Swiss Destiny Bernese Mountain Dogs

If you've shown your Berner that you can offer him the things that are essential for a safe, secure, and loving life, you will gain his respect. For dogs, it's all about the pack mentality. The leader of the pack is the one who has proven that he or she is capable of taking care of the rest of the pack. The dogs will look to Alpha Dog to take care of them and to teach them everything they need to know to ensure their survival. They will test the Alpha Dog periodically to see if he's still in charge. If they decide that he's no longer worthy of the respect of the other pack members, someone else will step up and take over. Your dog wants reassurance that you are, indeed, capable of assuming the position of leader of the pack. If not, he will be eager to take over the job.

Respect works both ways. Your dog needs his space, his privacy, and the opportunity to do what his doggy instincts tell him is natural in the dog world. So, unless he's doing something you find totally repulsive, give him respect by understanding that this is what dogs do. Yes, they sniff each other's butts. Your dog's dinner manners can be sloppy at best. He'll mark his territory. He's an animal, you're a human. Mutual respect should be practiced by even the youngest family members. If your dog is enjoying a good munch on a toy, don't allow a child to take it away from him. Pulling on a dog's fur, ears, or tail is never acceptable, nor is waking a dog when he is sleeping or bothering him when he is eating. No teasing, either. It's not just about training the dog. Sometimes it's about training the people, too.

Basic Commands

Once your Berner has had a chance to settle into his new environment, it's time to begin working with him on basic commands. There are seven that we'll concentrate on for now: Sit, Release, Down, Stay, Recall, Heel, and Drop/Leave it. Every trainer starts with Sit. It's the easiest for your dog to learn, and it's simple to reinforce throughout the day without too much effort. In preparation for most of the commands, you'll need some small treats that your dog finds tasty and a flat collar on your dog with a six-foot leash attached. It's important to note here that there are two very different types of treats that you can use when working with your Bernese: bite-sized training treats that he'll scoff down in an instant or "high-value treats", which can be used for enticing him to achieve more difficult commands. For now, a small treat that your dog can chew quickly and easily will be the best choice. You don't want him casually munching on something that takes a long time to eat as it will break his concentration on the training routine.

The Sit Command

- Standing in front of your dog with the leash in your hand, show him the treat, holding it only an inch or two from his nose.

- Slowly move the treat above his head, so that he's watching the treat, and in a quiet voice, say, "Sit."

- If he doesn't sit, gently move your hand down his back, guiding his butt to the floor.

- When he sits, immediately give him the treat, and say, "Good sit!" - and as always, lots of praise.

Your Berner may not grasp the concept right away, so continue working with him three or four times a day, five minutes at a time. If he's not paying attention, make sure there are no distractions. Take him into a quieter room where he can focus on you. Be sure the floor where you're working is comfortable for him. Some dogs will slide on a shiny, tile floor. Likewise, a stiff carpet may be the cause of inattention and discomfort. Does your dog love the treats you're using as rewards? If he's not thoroughly enjoying them, switch to something that he'll find more appealing. As your dog

Photo Courtesy of Sandy Wilburn

Photo Courtesy of Liz Smith

begins to understand the Sit command, you can use it throughout the day. Reinforce what he's learned by asking him to sit at the door before going outside. (If he's in a hurry to get outside for potty time, however, don't ask him to sit first. He may really, really need to get out there!)

You can also ask him to sit before putting the food bowl down for him. Keep the training short, simple, and praise and reward him when he's trying his best. After your dog understands the verbal Sit command, at some point you can begin using a hand signal...but let's save that for later. (The hand signal for Sit is just a small scooping motion with your hand from right to left.) You don't want to overwhelm him with too much information right now, so stick with voice commands for the time being. Did we mention, PRAISE and REWARD? Absolutely!

The OK a.k.a. the Release Command

Your dog needs a simple word that he'll recognize to know that he's "off duty" from his command. If you tell him to sit, for example, he'll very much appreciate knowing when it's the right time for him to get up, relax, chill out... hence, the Release command.

Find a word that works for you, which you can use with consistency. I use "OK" to let a dog know that his command has ended. You can also use "Release", "All done", "Free", or whatever word you prefer.

If you're just starting to work on commands with your dog, it's best to wait until he is thoroughly familiar with the Sit command before starting on Release. Again, don't confuse him by adding too much at once. Slow, steady, consistent, and a reward with praise and/or treats will do the trick. The Release command should have an enthusiastic tone to it, so your dog knows he has made you happy with his good efforts.

The Down Command

Now that your Berner knows how to sit upon command, you can begin working on Down. It won't be as easy for him to learn, so please don't become frustrated if it takes a while for him to understand what you're asking him to do. Some dogs see Down as a somewhat submissive stance, so be patient, keep your voice gentle, and give plenty of encouragement, praise, and rewards.

- Let your dog know that you have a treat for him and give him the Sit command.
- Place the treat a few inches from his nose; then, slowly lower the treat to the floor, all the while saying, "Down."
- See if he will lower his belly to the floor. If not, place your hand on his back between his shoulder blades and apply gentle pressure as you guide him down. Keep praising and encouraging him.

Photo Courtesy
of Maryellen Dolan

- It's easier to keep his flat collar on him with his six-foot leash, as you gently lower the leash towards the floor. Your efforts to get him into the Down position should be slow and with a calming voice.
- When your dog is in the Down position, offer abundant praise and a treat.
- When he's totally familiar with the verbal Down command, you can try adding the hand command for Down. Use a flat hand motion, palm facing downward, slightly lowering your hand towards the floor, while repeating the word "Down".
- Work in conjunction with the OK command to release him.

Your future objective will be to teach your Berner to go directly from a standing position to Down. Again, always use positive reinforcement, and keep your training sessions short and enjoyable. Training should be fun for everyone!

The Stay Command

You should never consider the Stay command optional. It could, in fact, be the one command that saves your dog's life. Picture this: You're walking with your dog in the park, and he's off leash. A squirrel crosses your path, and your beloved Berner takes off at breakneck speed after that squirrel, just as said rodent is bounding for the woods. Your dog needs to hear "STAY" as soon as this scenario begins to play out. Otherwise, will your dog continue into the woods? Will you find him again? It's a definite safety measure, so working with your Berner as early as possible on the Stay command should be part of essential training.

- Give your dog the Sit command. As you begin working on this command, you can use a flat collar and leash if you find it easier.
- Walk backwards a few feet away from him, all the while repeating, "Stay." If he gets up to follow you, bring the dog back to where he was sitting, and say, "Sit," then, "Stay."
    - o(For the Stay command, I use the hand command that I use to signal Stop - a flat palm out and facing your dog.)
- Walk backwards and a few feet away from him again. After a few seconds say, "OK" or whatever your Release word is, and praise and/or give him a treat.
    - oYou can put your dog on a Down instead of a Sit if it seems less stressful. I prefer to teach a dog Stay from the Down position as it's more comfortable for him. When he's proficient with the command, you can simply move to Stay from wherever and however he is positioned.

- Gradually, increase the length of time that he's in Stay.

- Praise should most definitely follow your dog's successful efforts. Even when you're confident that he understands the Stay, practice often with him, and reinforce the command.

Recall: *The Come Command*

The Recall (or Come) command is another order that your Berner MUST learn, and he must learn to respond quickly, no matter what the circumstances. Again, it could be a life saver. Having a dog who does not respond to your command of "Come" is potentially putting his (and possibly YOUR) life in danger. So, you must teach him the command in the most rewarding, fun, enthusiastic way so he doesn't hesitate for a second when called. Your Berner's mindset when working on the Recall should be that when he hears "Come", there will be the most wonderful reward or praise waiting when he reaches you. To teach this command, break out those high value, special treats that your dog absolutely loves and for which he will do anything. He needs to know that "Come!" means a totally spectacular reward is waiting.

About those high-value treats: Some dog trainers have reported significant success using cheese bits (especially string cheese cut into bite-sized pieces), small bits of cooked meat and chicken, and Cheerios breakfast cereal. The pieces are small, the dogs love them, and they won't add too many extra calories to your dog's daily diet.

- When you're ready to work on the Recall with your Berner, pick a time of day when he's relaxed, has no distractions (kids, toys, noise, etc.), and has already had his bathroom break.

- Bring your dog into a fairly roomy space where you can work with him uninterrupted.

- Put his flat collar and leash on him. Have his high-value treats handy.

- Give the commands to Sit and then Stay, followed by a treat and praise when he complies.

- Take a few steps backwards and give the command, "Come!" (The hand signal I use is a slight wave of my palm toward my chest area.)

- If the dog doesn't respond, walk toward him, pick up his leash, and walk backwards to the spot where you originally stood, all the while saying, "Come", in a calm, cheerful voice. Treat time!

- Next, have your Berner Sit and Stay in that spot, drop the leash, walk away, and repeat.

Do not praise him or offer a treat if he only gets halfway to you; instead, encourage him to come all the way. He needs to be within arm's reach.

Practice, practice, but only as long as your dog is interested and responsive. If he's getting tired or not focusing, take a break and come back to it at a later time. Don't give up. Your Bernese Mountain Dog can be pretty darned stubborn when he wants to be. He's smart, but you're smarter. Plus, you've got the treats.

When you're confident that he understands the Recall, it's time to take things outside where there is a plethora of smells, sounds, and everything that makes life interesting for your Berner. Your job is to get him to focus on YOU. To assist in this new endeavor, use the following:

- Attach a long rope (twenty feet or so) to your dog's collar.

- Ask him to sit and stay, giving a treat when he complies.

- Now, walk to the end of the rope and say, "Come." If he's not responding or is too busy checking out the surrounding scenery, you can gently reel him in toward you, all the while saying, "Come."

- When he's within arm's reach, praise and offer that special treat.

Remember, it's not easy for your dog to multi-task: there's a bird chirping somewhere down the street, there's a mail truck approaching, the neighbors are out watering their lawn, and you're asking your Berner to come to your side, all at the same time. When he does what you need him to do, give him another treat and some extra special praise. He has just completed a job that required an exorbitant amount of attention on his part, so let him know you're happy with the effort involved. It wasn't easy.

A cautionary word here: Do not, under any circumstances, allow your dog off leash (unless he's in an enclosed area) until you are 100% sure that you can trust his Recall! It may take months of work. A dog who responds to Come 99% of the time is a dog who should still be on a leash when taking walks, playing outside, or enjoying outings. That 1% of the time is 1% too many. Don't take the risk.

The Heel Command

I don't often use the Heel command with my dog because I usually find it unnecessary. Our walks are fairly casual and unhurried, so it's not something we focus on. My dog is much happier to be sniffing hydrants, meeting new friends, and looking to mark "that perfect spot" that will tell her four-legged acquaintances, "I was here." However, she knows what the command means, and she will Heel if asked.

If you're not sure what the Heel command should look like, think of the professional dog show competitions you've seen on television. The handlers run with their dogs positioned by their immediate side. When the handler stops, the dog stops and sits. It's a thing of beauty to watch. If you don't plan to show your dog in competition, why would you need to practice the Heel? Here's one reason:

I live on the North Shore of the Boston area, and winters here get messy. With snow piles and limited sidewalk access, we hearty New Englanders occasionally do need to implement the Heel command for our dogs. When walkways are icy, or if you've got physical limitations, you don't want a pulling dog to be the cause of your emergency trip to the hospital. So, if your dog tends to pull on his leash, even the slightest tug can mean trouble for you.

Aside from a physical risk, when you ask your Berner to Heel, you're reinforcing your Alpha Dog status. You ask, he complies. Heeling will also contribute to your dog's mental stimulation. He's exercising his brain and thinking about what he should be doing. If you have practiced this command with your dog enough, chances are good that he won't be tempted to pull ahead of you on walks. Here's how to practice the Heel command:

- As with other training sessions, begin working in a quiet environment with no distractions.

- Have a collar and leash on your dog and carry some training treats.

- Walk with your dog close by your side with no slack in the leash. You want him next to your leg.

- Repeat the command, "Heel" as you walk; then, stop quickly. Give the Sit command and when he sits, give him a treat and praise.

- Tell him "OK" (or whatever your Release word is), and as he gets up, immediately say "Heel", and repeat by walking with him at your side.

Keep it fun so that your dog is enjoying the process and use plenty of treats and praise. It will most likely take some time for him to completely understand, but when you're convinced that he's "got it", start working outside. If you use just a few Heel commands every time you go for a stroll, he'll always be ready to walk at your side. One additional note: All training should be done with a six-foot leash. Please don't even THINK of using a retractable leash for any of the training commands.

Some trainers will insist that dogs must heel on the handler's left side. Why?

Tradition! Heeling is thought to have originated many, many years ago, when hunters would train their dogs to stay on their left side for the simple reason that they carried their guns on their right side. For me, it depends upon which side of the street I'm walking on, as I prefer to have my dog heel on the side away from traffic. If you're more comfortable with your Berner walking on one side or the other, rest assured that the Heeling Police will probably not issue your dog a ticket for non-compliance.

The Drop It Command

This command is NOT an option. Every dog needs to respond to "Drop it." (You may also substitute "Leave it.") Whether your dog is munching on a toy, a tasty but potentially poisonous morsel that he's just dug up from your garden, or your expensive new leather clutch purse, "Drop it" should be an essential training command in your pet's vocabulary. In his mind, this command will once again reinforce your status as Top Dog, but it also may save his life (and possibly the life of your new purse).

- Give your dog a toy or something that catches his interest but not anything as enjoyable as his favorite training treat.

- When he's fully focused on the toy say, "Drop it," offer him a treat instead, and when he does drop the toy, give him some enthusiastic praise and the special treat.

This command will take some practice, but your dog will soon understand. Never pull the toy out of his mouth; he should let go of it willingly... because Big Dog said so.

CHAPTER 12
Physical and Mental Exercise

"Berners like to sleep a lot and they don't have much endurance when it comes to play sessions. If you notice your puppy trying to hide under a table, or behind furniture you may want to let your puppy have their space and get the rest they need. Sometimes we try to do too much to entertain our puppies and we could actually be over stimulating them."

ROBIN WORTS
Swiss Destiny Bernese Mountain Dogs

Photo Courtesy
of Crizelle Ilejay

Photo Courtesy
of Holley Makela

s a working breed, Bernese Mountain Dogs are quite happy when given a job to do. They love learning commands when training sessions are brief, and the process is fun. However, the lesson doesn't end with the sit, down, release, come, stay, heel, and drop it commands. Berners need physical AND mental exercises that will keep them busy and challenged. Boredom is the enemy of the Berner, and your dog's inactivity can lead to digging, aggression, behavioral problems, barking, and separation anxiety. That doesn't mean you have to provide constant entertainment, but your dog does need extra attention to keep him out of trouble.

Photo Courtesy of Katie Walther

Fun and Games for Your Berner

- Berners learn easily, so teach your dog the names of favorite toys. "Get your bunny," "Get your tennis ball," etc.

- Hide treats under plastic cups and say, "Find it!" Rotate the cups and try to confuse him. We'll bet he won't be fooled!

- Hide some treats or toys around the house for a rousing game of hide and seek. Key words here again, "Find it!"

- Dogs love bubbles, so head to the Dollar Store and buy a few bottles.

- If your Berner enjoys the water, purchase a plastic kiddie pool for him, fill it up, and with your supervision, let him chill out in his very own pool on hot days.

- A game of Fetch or Frisbee will keep your Berner amused for hours or for as long as your arm holds out. My throwing arm will definitely not qualify me for a spot in any Major League Baseball line up, but an inexpensive ball-chucker got my Berner running like a champ.

An internet search for "interactive dog toys" will produce a wealth of choices - from doggy versions of the old "Bop the Gopher" game to automatic treat dispensers.

How are you going to keep your dog's (many) toys from being scattered all over the house? With a doggy toy box, of course. Soft-sided boxes made specifically for your pooch's favorite possessions are an inexpensive solution to the doggy-toy clutter problem. You can also make a game of teaching him to pick up his toys and place them in the box himself.

Most Berners are fairly athletic creatures; however, if your new dog is a puppy, you'll need to start slowly. We've noted previously that a Bernese Mountain Dog does not mature as quickly as other breeds, so your dog's bones and joints will still be growing even though he may appear to be fully grown. While you don't need to live in a state of fear that every movement will cause skeletal or muscular damage to your dog, you should always provide him with age-appropriate exercise and activity.

Likewise, for a senior dog. Aching joints aren't just for elderly humans, so consider your dog's overall health when indulging in physical activities. Consulting with your veterinarian is the best course of action.

CHAPTER 13
The Importance of Socializing Your Berner

"BMD's are usually really good with other dogs. I would start off when they are young meeting dogs that are well behaved and not too rambunctious at first. Gradually ease your way into other dogs with varying energy levels. When your dog is meeting another dog it is best to put the leashes down and let them drag them around. Tension at the end of the leash from the dogs trying to sniff each other can send a negative message to the dog and make them feel unsafe or defensive. If the meeting doesn't go well you'll still be able to grab the leash off the ground and retrieve your dog quickly."

ROBIN WORTS
Swiss Destiny Bernese Mountain Dogs

Photo Courtesy
of Laura Orsini

Bernese Mountain Dogs need socialization from an early age and this should remain an ongoing component of their lives. Typically, Bernese Mountain Dogs show a natural curiosity about the world around them and are eager to explore. Meeting, greeting, and venturing into the unknown should be gradually encouraged. The key word here is "gradually." Berners are so appealing that most folks will naturally gravitate toward their happy-go-lucky presence. Your dog should be reassuringly inspired to check out unfamiliar faces and places, but he should never be forced to do so.

FUN FACT
Grief Support Dog

A funeral home in Pennsylvania is home to a unique grief support spokesperson. Mochi, a Bernese Mountain Dog, joined the staff at Macon Funeral Home in Franklin, Pennsylvania, in 2020 and is currently in training to become a grief therapy dog. Bernese Mountain Dogs make excellent therapy dogs because of their affectionate and gentle personalities.

Some Berners are more timid than others, so respect their cautionary nature. To let my dog know that it's alright for her to meet a new person, I simply say, "Friend." My dog then knows it's safe, and she can go sniff, check out someone whom she's never met, and slather them with doggy kisses if she's so inclined. In my experience, I've found that younger puppies are accepting of most people, but often an older dog will be more wary of strangers. If your dog is a rescue or has not been properly socialized, he may act in a reserved manner. Depending upon the experiences he had in his previous home, he could be harboring some aggressive tendencies, fears, or shyness. If your Berner negatively remembers someone in his past who had specific physical traits - a tall man with a beard, a woman who carried a large purse, or children who may have mistreated him, for example, your dog may shy away from or growl at someone with similar characteristics. His natural instincts will signal him to be cautious or to act in an aggressive or timid manner. In this case, consulting with a dog behavioral specialist may help.

Every dog, no matter what the age, should be taught the proper etiquette of how to behave in social situations. A Berner who jumps on people, barks, growls, counter surfs, begs at the dinner table, or exhibits other behaviors that are unacceptable needs instruction on proper doggy etiquette. When your dog is behaving in a disrespectful way, you need to step in and correct those bad manners. It all boils down to good socialization skills and proper training.

Introducing your Bernese Mountain Dog to New People, Places, and Things

"BMDs require moderate exercise. Walks and hikes are a wonderful way to get you and your pal out! Just take it slow while they are in their developmental stage. The BMD is more about the emotional connection than the mental stimulation. They are not typically a breed that needs to be kept busy to stay out of trouble. Continued education is always fun though and a great way to interact. All they truly seem to want is to be with you and be happily loved."

DIANE CALDEMEYER REID

Faraway Farms Inc

Photo Courtesy
of Eleanor Mitchell

Photo Courtesy
of Brian St.Onge

The world can be a frightening place for a Berner puppy, so the appropriate time to begin letting him know that it's not so scary out there is between the ages of four weeks and four months old. At this stage in his life, your responsibility will be to introduce him to the universe in a gentle, pleasant, fun way.

First, always check with your veterinarian to be sure that your puppy has had all necessary vaccinations for him to be exposed to other dogs and the new experiences that await. Your pup may exhibit various reactions that could cause you to scratch your head in wonder: "He's afraid of the wind?" or "He heard a car horn beep, and he started whimpering?" or "A chipmunk ran by and he was terrified?" Yes, indeed. These are all new experiences for your Berner, and there's no telling how he will respond. On the other hand, you may have that precious pup who is bothered by nothing. You will find out soon enough.

Your attitude toward new situations will tell your dog everything he needs to know. Stay upbeat, encouraging, and slowly expose your Berner to new experiences. Keep him leashed, have a pocketful of small treats, and begin to positively reinforce his response to everything that's unfamiliar.

Build his confidence to explore, but don't overwhelm him. If he seems fearful, don't coddle him, but let him know in a gentle manner that he is safe.

Although remaining watchful of your dog's response to new situations is important, what many dog owners don't comprehend is that a dog is an expert at interpreting what's going on at the other end of his leash. That's YOU. Consider this: If you and your Berner are out walking and encounter another dog walker, you may automatically tense up and pull back (even slightly) on the leash. Your dog immediately thinks, DANGER! It doesn't take very much for your Bernese, no matter how young or old, to understand the signals that you're sending. You may not realize it, but he certainly does. Watch his reaction but be aware of your own as well.

Puppy Socialization/Kindergarten Classes

"Puppy classes are a great way to safely socialize your pup! Bernese are typically very social with other dogs. They do not tend towards aggression. It is however important to be very aware of the dogs that they are meeting. Some older dogs do not take to puppies sniffing and checking their underside for food. So go slow and watch behaviors carefully."

DIANE CALDEMEYER REID

Faraway Farms Inc.

Kindergarten classes for puppies? That's ridiculous, you may think. Not so fast. Consider how much a child learns in their first year of school: Meeting new friends, learning how to play in a group, respecting others' property, good manners, and listening to the teacher. Puppy Kindergarten will also teach your dog these concepts...and more. Puppy Kindergarten is an excellent, affordable means of getting your dog off to a successful start in life.

A well-socialized dog will be a wonderful addition to your family. You won't be casting a cautious eye on him whenever an unfamiliar dog approaches or a stranger stops by to admire your Bernese. This training will ease the tension of not knowing how your dog will react. Will he growl? Bark? Bite? An improperly socialized dog will create worry that will follow you everywhere for a long, long time. Puppy socialization classes are a wonderful investment.

Classes are offered at many locations. Big-box pet stores, doggy day care centers, and canine-training facilities run organized and supervised Puppy Kindergartens. Ask dog owner friends for recommendations; often veterinarians will know of classes in your area, too. Although puppy groups may differ in how they are run, the basic premise is to provide young dogs with the opportunity to socialize and play with others who are of a similar age and maturity. Some groups will allow a pet parent to visit a class in progress, without bringing their dog along for a first visit, just to observe

*Photo Courtesy
of Brian Beardsley*

how everything works. Groups are run by trainers and facilitators who are familiar with dog socialization and who usually begin working with the dogs on basic commands. The group leaders may also give a general assessment of each dog's personality as they interact with the group. Most classes meet once a week for approximately six to eight weeks.

You'll also have a chance to meet with other puppy parents, ask questions of the group facilitator, and your Berner will have a fun time and burn off some of that puppy energy. If you have concerns about your dog's behavior, the group leader should be able to answer some generic questions, or if need be, refer you to more advanced classes or possibly a dog behavioral specialist. You'll also have an opportunity to do what every pet parent (and human parent) excels in - comparing your little cherub to others in the group. Is your dog outgoing? Shy? Does he show Leader of the Doggy Pack potential, or is he more laid back and happy to follow that sweet, little Golden Retriever pup around? At the very least, your Berner will be ready for a nice, long nap when he gets home.

Socializing Your Older Bernese Mountain Dog with Other Dogs

"With older Berners, meet on neutral territory, keep leashes loose (tension on the lead from you tells your dogs to worry about the other dog) or parallel walk. Berners are mostly good with other dogs, but some have dog aggression issues with certain breeds."

BARB WALTENBERRY
Barberry BMD

There can be some challenges involved when socializing an older dog. If he has never had a chance to be with other dogs or was neglected and abused, it will be up to you to take things slowly and calmly. Start by taking your dog for long walks and acclimating him, in a controlled way and on a short leash, to social situations. He'll enjoy expending some energy while still being able to meet other dogs, and it will allow you to work on some basic commands. Keep your demeanor casual but pay close attention to how he responds. If you meet someone walking their dog, always ask if their pet is friendly before letting the animals get close to one another. Some dogs can be friendly when off leash and on neutral territory, but they might become aggressive toward another dog when both are on leash. Depending upon

Photo Courtesy
of Blair Johnson

the dog, they might think they are protecting you, or they might perceive the other dog as a threat to their own safety. If you don't know your dog's personality yet, go slowly.

Read your dog's body language and get to know your Berner's physical cues. I cringe every time someone looks at my dog and says, "Oh! She's wagging her tail. She must be happy!" A wagging tail is not always the sign of a happy dog. It usually is, but it could also mean that he's nervous, agitated, or afraid. Obvious signs of an anxious dog: his tail is tucked between his legs, the hairs on his neck and back stand up, he bares his teeth, he growls or pants, his ears are pulled back, or he is trembling. If your dog exhibits any of these behaviors, calmly remove him from the situation.

Some dogs have issues with certain types of dogs. Your dog may adore dogs his own size or smaller, but he could be terrified of bigger dogs. Some dogs are more aggressive toward dogs of the same or opposite sex or of males that have not been neutered. Older dogs, or dogs with health issues, could have little tolerance for young puppies. Learn what your dog's body language is saying, and if it's a reminder of an unpleasant experience from his past, be mindful that just one minor incident could set him off. Respect his feelings, consult with a specialist if necessary, and work toward a successful socialization experience.

Socializing Your Berner with People

Every dog has his own unique personality. Your dog may be shy and timid and take a few steps backward when meeting strangers. He could become the canine-version of a Velcro strap and attach himself to your leg! On the other hand, he may be the first to forge ahead to say hello. The rules of socializing your dog with people are basically the same rules that apply to introducing him to other dogs: exposure, exposure, exposure. The more people he gets to meet, the more your dog will understand that the world is not so scary. Let him go at his own pace, and don't force him to like everyone.

I don't particularly care if my dog doesn't like everyone. I don't like everyone, either. Some people wave hello and stop to chat with me when we're out walking while others keep going without a smile or an acknowledgement of my presence. Of course, I'm not about to growl at strangers or threaten them in any way. I know enough to be pleasant, at the very least, and to not provoke any confrontations. This should apply to your dog as well. He doesn't need to greet everyone with hand licks and tail wags, but proper etiquette dictates that he should at least not instigate a brawl. At a minimum, it's essential for him to be polite.

In addition to organized play groups, there are a host of opportunities to socialize your dog. Most pet stores allow leashed dogs in their establishments. It's a good place to expose your dog to other dogs in a controlled atmosphere. As a new pet owner, you'll probably be visiting those stores often, and for your dog, it will be a brand-new experience. Plus, your Berner may enjoy picking out his own treats!

Outdoor activities such as country fairs, concerts in the park, neighborhood gatherings, and farmers markets will give your dog a chance to socialize with other pets and their people. Take advantage of pleasant weather and special occasions to have your Berner accompany you to other dog-friendly events. A pocketful of treats + lots of praise = a happy dog and a happy dog parent. Remember, though, that not everyone loves dogs, and not every place welcomes them.

CHAPTER 14

Benefits of Doggy Day Care for Socialization

I love doggy day care. My dog loves doggy day care. The doggy day care staff loves my dog. What's not to love? Well, a few things. First, your dog must be a suitable candidate for doggy day care. Next, you must be confident that the day care establishment that you're considering will be committed to keeping your dog safe, and your dog must enjoy spending time there. Your Berner will get plenty of interaction with other dogs and staff members and have a few hours of fun. He'll build his social skills and come home tired from a hard day's play. As his dog parent, the benefits are many: You can have some time for yourself without having to run home to take your pooch out to relieve himself. You won't worry that he's been home alone for too long. You'll know that he's enjoying himself, isn't bored, and hasn't resorted to chewing up your Oriental carpet.

Photo Courtesy
of Kimberley Rice

Although it may seem like it's all fun and games, if the day care facility isn't a good fit for your dog, you'll need to find a different establishment or look for an alternative care provider. Not every dog enjoys doggy day care. Dogs who are extremely timid, aggressive, older, and physically frail, or who have never been socialized might not do well. Doggy day care centers can be overwhelming, noisy, and overly stimulating due to the constant activity. In this case, a smaller day care facility or private home day care might be a better choice. Shorter day care sessions may be an alternative as well. If you're away during the day and your dog is happier hanging out at home, hiring a dog walker could be a great solution so your dog can continue to lounge on the sofa and to take a few leisurely walks while you're away.

How to Choose a Doggy Day Care Facility

There are numerous doggy day care facilities in most communities. With so many choices when considering an establishment, what should you look for? Here's a short checklist:

- Get referrals. Talk with your veterinarian and other dog parents who use day care; visit the facilities first without your dog.
- What's your overall impression? Is the facility clean?
- Is the staff certified (may vary by state) well-trained, caring, knowledgeable, and friendly?
- Are they happy to answer any questions that you have?
- How long have they been in business?
- What experience do they have with Bernese Mountain Dogs?
- How many dogs do they care for on a typical day?
- Is it well supervised, and what is the human-to-dog ratio?
- Are smaller dogs and bigger dogs kept separately? (The answer to that question should be a resounding "YES." You don't want your young puppy in with a 150-pound Mastiff, no matter how friendly the big fellow might be. Injuries can happen, however unintentional.)
- Many doggy day care centers have fenced, outdoor facilities, so in good weather, the dogs can be out in the fresh air. (My dog loves to be in the water and will spend hours in the summer just hanging out in the kiddie pool provided by the staff.)
- Are the play areas large enough to handle a large number of dogs?

- Are there spaces where dogs can go for some quiet time when they need to relax?

- What are the hours of operation? Is there a half-day option? (Some dogs just don't do well in an all-day situation. A long, tiring day - no matter how much fun - can cause your dog some stress if he's not used to that much activity.)

Photo Courtesy
of Toni Carver

- Does the facility have overnight and/or extended boarding, and is there someone who stays with the boarders all night?
- Do the dogs have a schedule during the day? (Many facilities follow set times for rest periods in order to keep dogs from becoming overly stimulated from too much play.)
- What are the pricing options, and do they offer any cost-effective packages for frequent day care?
- Do they have "drop-in" options, where you can bring your dog for an hour or so at a lesser cost?
- Are they bonded and insured?
- What health certificates do they require, and how often must these be updated?
- Are there spay and neuter requirements?
- What procedures are implemented in case a dog is injured?
- Do they offer grooming and training?
- Is the facility heated and air conditioned?

Many centers now offer a video stream, so you can check, by using your home computer or mobile device, to see what your dog is doing. It's great to pop in for a virtual visit once in a while, but we'd caution you that too much viewing time is not a good idea. Dogs have their own language, and what you might interpret as aggressiveness may simply be that this is how your Bernese Mountain Dog and his friends are playing. If the technology is available, that's nice, but please don't turn into a virtual helicopter dog parent and hover over your pooch.

Sure, there's a lot of information, but researching is the best way to find a facility where your dog will be happy, and you'll be comfortable knowing that your Berner is safe and secure.

Visiting the Day Care and Completing Applications

If you've decided that a doggy day care center would benefit your dog, you'll be invited to bring him in for an initial evaluation. Staff members will ask you to fill out an application with pertinent information regarding your dog's personality and history. Before the evaluation takes place, you will need to provide a copy of your dog's vaccination and medical information.

The staff will put your dog through some paces to see how he responds. Is he shy? Nervous? Or is he ready to get in there and make some new friends?

You will usually be asked to leave your dog for a period of time, which could vary from an hour to a half day. (Many facilities will offer the evaluation and first visit at no charge.) The staff will typically bring in one of their more

Photo Courtesy of Calli Borutski

laid-back, regular client dogs or a staff member's dog for a meet and greet to see how your dog responds. They will evaluate for sociability, aggressiveness, submissiveness, and overall temperament. If it's a "go," your dog will be welcome to come play and to enjoy all that doggy day care has to offer; however, if it's a "no", don't take it personally. A responsible doggy day care facility will not accept a dog if there's even the slightest chance that he may be putting himself or other dogs at risk. A well-run, conscientious, professional center would rather turn a prospective client away than put any of their dogs in danger.

Decision Time and Final Thoughts

If doggy day care is a good fit for your dog, there's one more bit of advice: Be sure your Berner receives regular flea and tick preventative treatments and is up to date on kennel cough and flu shots. No matter how clean or conscientious a doggy day care provider is, diseases and infestations can still be spread from one dog to another. Some, but not all, doggy day care facilities require these preventative measures, while for other facilities, it's optional.

Not every doggy day care will be a good match for every dog. My own pup, who is one of the sweetest, most laid-back dogs I've ever owned, was turned down at a local doggy day care center after her initial evaluation. The reason? She wasn't aggressive, her behavior was fine, but she "really didn't contribute much to the pack." Well then. We tried another day care center, where she was evaluated, welcomed with open paws, and she's been a once or twice a week regular there for seven years. She loves going there, and they love having her. She fits in nicely, she comes home tired after a day of fun, and is a happy girl.

If you think that your Berner just wouldn't be well-suited in a doggy day care setting, there are alternatives. Professional dog walkers are available in most neighborhoods, providing services for both private and group walks. Some walkers will even take their doggy clients for hikes in the woods, to the beach, or on field trips. Private dog play-group providers are also available in some communities, allowing four or five dogs to spend time together in home settings. For those dogs who enjoy some canine companionship, but on a quieter and more limited basis, this may be the perfect choice. Again, it's just as important to check references, experience, cleanliness, supervision, insurance and bonding, necessary health certifications, rules and regulations, and safety measures. No matter which method of dog care you're considering as the best for you and your Berner, trust your instincts. If something just doesn't seem right, listen to your inner Momma Dog!

CHAPTER 15
Do You Need a Professional Dog Trainer?

"Study up on positive training methods. Berners will not learn from negatives, it is all about positives and quality time spent with them. They learn quickly especially if you make a big fuss over them about how smart they are. You will literally see them 'smile' when praised and they know they have made you happy."

AMY KESSLER
Lionheart Bernese

Photo Courtesy
of Tamara Stephenson

You and your new dog are most likely off to a great start, and by now, you've probably both settled into a nice, comfortable routine. Mr. Berner is sweet, loving, and you and your family adore him, and he loves his humans. The training process is going well, and there are no issues. There appears to be nothing out of the ordinary with your dog's behavior. Oh, sure, every now and then your Berner might slip up a bit. Someone rings the doorbell, and the dog barks to alert you that there's a visitor. You tell the dog, "No barking," but for some reason known only to him, he just has to get in one last bark after you've asked him to stop. The next time this scene plays out, it's two more barks, then three. Basically, he's ignoring

Photo Courtesy of Sheryl Carbone

you, thumbing his nose at Momma Dog, and in his own way, telling you he'll do what he darned well pleases. To you, it may not seem like a big deal, but to him, well...Score one for the Dog Team! And so, it begins.

Putting Your Pooch Before Your Pride

Are you under the impression that dog trainers are only for dogs with serious behavioral issues? Do you think that calling a professional trainer is the equivalent of admitting that you're failing in your efforts to raise the perfect pooch? Neither is the case. It just means that your Berner is doing what every dog does - he's testing you. And you're doing what many dog parents do - allowing him to push the limits. While many professional dog trainers and dog behavioral specialists do work with dogs with serious issues, there are many more who specialize in teaching pet parents how to address those smaller, quirky, every day annoyances that a good majority of new dog owners experience. Little concerns have a habit of growing into much bigger problems. Sometimes you just need a bit of help.

Behaviors Which May Indicate Professional Help is Needed

Here are a few behaviors that you may have noticed as they pertain to your dog; some might sound quite familiar. If so, and you're not sure how to improve the situation, a professional dog trainer could be the answer.

A professional dog trainer can help with the following problems:

- There are issues with your dog's potty training.
- This is your first dog, and you're not sure if what you're doing is correct. You just need some guidance.
- You'd like your dog to be more sociable with people and other dogs.

Additionally, a professional trainer may be able to help in the following situations:

- Doesn't pay attention to you when you need him to respond.
- Ignores your corrections.
- Seems to have forgotten his commands.
- Constantly gets into trouble, tearing up the house, eating things he shouldn't be eating like shoes, furniture, etc.
- Won't let anyone near him when he's eating.
- Barks too much.
- Howls when you leave him alone.
- Is pushy with other dogs.
- Jumps on everyone.
- Is so happy to see visitors at your door that he greets them by urinating.
- Is afraid of everything.
- Play-bites and nips at the kids.
- Counter surfs and steals food.
- Begs at the table.
- Growls at people and/or other dogs.
- Is older and has some odd behaviors.

Here's the bottom line: If your dog is acting in a manner which is displeasing to you and your family, there's no good reason to delay in seeking assistance from a professional. You can try to rationalize your dog's behavior by saying, "Oh, he's just a puppy. He'll grow out of it." or "We adopted him,

and he must have had a bad upbringing." or "He's too old to learn anything new. We'll just deal with it." There should be no excusing your dog's behavioral issues or bad manners. Get thee to a trainer!

Finding the Right Professional Dog Trainer

How did you find the right dog? You may have asked friends or checked with a veteri nary practice for referrals. Maybe you did a comprehensive internet search. Your research to find a trainer should follow the same route. Don't rule out checking with staff at dog shelters and rescue organizations. The quest to re-home a dog often involves training to alleviate certain behavioral problems before a dog can be placed in a new home, so shelter and rescue people are usually familiar with trainers who work with specific dog traits. Don't hesitate to call area dog organizations as well as breed clubs for recommendations.

Finding a knowledgeable dog trainer is obviously important, but finding the right trainer is essential. Do you need to concentrate on proper doggy etiquette? Is there a major issue such as aggression? Do your homework and find a professional who can best address your concerns and whose specialty applies to your dog's specific needs.

Photo Courtesy of Kathleen Schell

Questions to Ask a Prospective Dog Trainer

- What is your specialty?
- What experience and education in dog training do you have?
- Are you certified or hold any licenses? (Note: Most states do not require dog trainers to be certified or licensed. However, there are numerous certifications and professional organizations which offer membership to trainers in order to encourage development and to further career opportunities; they also offer ongoing education for trainers to help them maintain high standards within the industry.)
- What are your training methods and philosophy?
- Do you have experience working with Bernese Mountain Dogs?
- Is there an initial evaluation?
- What is the cost for training sessions?

- Will you be working with me (and my family) to teach us how to train the dog?
- Do you encourage all family members (and/or young children) to be present at training sessions?
- Approximately how many sessions will we need?
- Do you offer group or individual classes?
- Where does the training take place?
- Can you train my dog at my home?
- Do you provide training indoors or outdoors?
- Is there a class size limit?
- At what age do you recommend training should begin?
- Do you have experience working with an older dog, if applicable?
- Are there any guarantees?
- What equipment will we need to purchase?
- If your dog has a specific behavioral issue, ask what experience the trainer has in working with that issue.

Make your own list of questions and consider your priorities. Don't be afraid to ask before you commit to working with a trainer. A good trainer will always be happy to answer your questions, explain their methods and philosophy, and will want you to feel comfortable and understand the process.

The most important aspect of any dog training program is the dog owner. You can send your dog off to a training camp or program, but you must also understand what you will need to do to ensure that your dog continues to be the best that he can be. You cannot assume that just because your Berner has had three or ten or twenty sessions with a dog trainer, he'll automatically know how to behave. He won't, and even if he does, if you don't know what you're supposed to be doing, your dog's new knowledge will be short lived. Your professional dog trainer should be just as interested in teaching you everything you need to know to work with your dog in order to continue

CELEBRITY DOGS

Klueso Kapel

Klueso Kapel is an Instagram-famous Bernese Mountain Dog living in Perth, Australia. With over 67,000 followers, Klueso's adventures are seen and enjoyed by many. From beachside frolics to backyard playdates, it's clear that Klueso enjoys a good life.

that training. If you have others living in the household, they, too, should be encouraged to participate in training sessions. Fifty percent of the work that a professional dog trainer does is with your dog. The other fifty percent should be in working with you.

Puppy Obedience Training Classes and Beyond

We've already discussed Puppy Kindergarten, but those classes focus primarily on socialization for your young pooch. After Kindergarten groups, your dog should be enrolled in the next phase - Puppy Obedience Training. Classes will usually address general concerns pertinent to young dogs such as play-biting and nipping, excessive chewing, jumping, house training, and general obedience. The class facilitator/trainer should offer suggestions and demonstrate how to work on basic commands such as Sit, Down, Come, Drop It, walking on a leash, and Heel. Most puppy classes are offered for dogs between eight to sixteen weeks of age. The number of sessions will vary - most often between four to six classes, and you should be required to show proof of initial vaccinations in order to register your dog.

This is the age when your puppy is learning so much, and it's the best time to continually reinforce all his - and your - new knowledge. Work with your dog on an ongoing basis and keep your at-home training sessions short but frequent. Give your dog plenty of positive feedback, small treats, and praise as rewards, and above all, make it enjoyable for both of you. Training your pup can be a wonderful bonding experience.

Dealing with Your Berner's "Teenage Phase"

Bernese Mountain Dogs are known to mature slower, both physically and mentally, than other breeds, so while your dog may appear to be fully grown at the age of eight to twelve months, he's not quite there yet. He may appear gangly, clumsy, or awkward. His body is still developing, his hormones are running rampant, and his brain...well, let's just say, he's a typical teenager – unpredictable and perhaps moody one minute and happy the next. So, be aware that change is in the air. He's still the lovable, sweet, goofy guy that he's always been, but there will be times when you'll look at him and ask, "What the heck were you thinking?" This is not the time to let up on training.

Congratulations - you are now the proud parent of an adolescent dog. It will be a challenging time for both you and your Berner. Watch for changes beginning at approximately nine months. Usually by eighteen months, you'll have your always sweet, adorable guy back.

There's no telling what to expect during this phase of his life, but rest assured, it won't be a stage that will last forever - as long as you're aware of what your dog is going through at the moment and are committed to working with him. Again, with positive reinforcement, consistency, routine, patience, and lots of love, you'll both survive the teenage period of his life.

Both male and female Berners will experience physical as well as emotional changes during this time, with females going into heat and males marking their territory by lifting their legs to urinate. In both sexes, aggressive tendencies may develop.

Unless you are planning to breed your dog, follow your veterinarian's recommendations for the best time to spay or neuter. It's generally believed that dogs who are spayed or neutered have much less chance of developing cancers, urinary tract infections, and they have a longer life expectancy than unsterilized dogs. Often, besides the elimination of territorial marking and aggression, roaming and behavioral issues may also be greatly diminished.

Your teenage dog is now at the stage where he's starting to question your authority and having second thoughts about everything you've ever taught him: "So, how come YOU'RE big dog?...You're not the boss of me!...There's a dog over there, and I need to go check him out....Just because you're asking me to sit, doesn't mean I have to...Oh, treats. No big deal. I'd rather go sniff that tree...Think I'll go terrorize the cat..."

My own Berner, Moxie, acquired the title of Teen Terror right on schedule at nine months of age. She was a textbook doggy adolescent. Good behavior became a thing of the past and former misdemeanors became felonies. In what seemed like an overnight transformation, I saw months of training disappear as she "forgot" commands, foraged into trash bins, dug holes in the yard, and barked incessantly. My adorable, little princess was now a royal pain in the butt. It was time to kick her training routine into high gear. It took a while, but eventually, my little blockhead Berner returned to Magnificent Moxie mode. Her training became a life-long learning experience for both of us.

You need not agonize over your dog's behavior no matter what his age or stage in development. Help is available, so find a dog trainer who fits your needs. Research, interview, ask questions. Be honest in your assessment of your dog's behavior, and let the trainer know what your concerns are. Together, you can make it work.

Well-behaved Berners make wonderful therapy dogs. If you envision having your pet accompany you to schools, assisted living residences, nursing homes, hospitals, and other facilities where sociable and respectful canines are welcome, I encourage you to learn what opportunities and requirements are available. Your pooch will be admired for his amazing people skills, and what better way to bring a bit of happiness to someone who might not have had a reason to smile lately?

CHAPTER 16

Dealing With Unwanted Behavior – Your Dog's Bad Habits

"If a Berner doesn't get enough attention or gets bored, they will get mischievous. They tend to chew things and dig holes. Just give them as much attention as possible and if that doesn't work, try giving them a job. They are working dogs and like to be useful. Teach them to pull a cart, take them to classes and teach them new things. Teach them to retrieve the paper or get things for you in the house. While you are teaching them and working with them, you are also spending valuable time with them, which is what they want anyway. It's a win-win situation."

MELINDA SUTTON
Beth's Bernies

Photo Courtesy
of David and Anna Guilford

Many dog owners are guilty of covering up for their dog's poor choices and bad manners. We brush those infractions aside and blame ourselves for being too tired, too busy, or...well, just plain lazy when it comes to working with our pet. You may rationalize that your dog is smart, and he'll get it eventually. You'll tell yourself, "It's just a phase. It's the kids' fault. They shouldn't have teased him. He's just barking because he's being protective. Oh, yes, he cries and howls when we leave him home alone, but he's lonely." Then, one day, you'll wonder why the dog is out of control. Why is he barking/growling/digging/jumping/whining/nipping? It's because he can. You have become an enabler.

Photo Courtesy of Brian Stephens

Let's work on correcting a few common dog misbehaviors.

Chewing

Puppies are notorious chewers. They're not particularly discriminating about what goes into their mouths, and if an item carries the scent of their dog parent or a family member, all the better. Shoes, underwear, socks all have bizarre appeal to a young pup. His gums are sore, new teeth are coming in, and chewing feels really, really good.

Hopefully, by now you've been working with your dog on the Drop it/ Leave it command. If he's chewing random objects, this is the perfect time to start reinforcing. Do not use a treat for this one, however, because it could backfire. Here's why: Mr. Smarty-pants Berner will reason that, "Every time I find something to chew on that I shouldn't have, they'll give me a treat instead! Wow, I am so smart!"

Your own reasoning should that he needs to drop it because you said so. Praise him when he gives up those boxer shorts, but don't make too big of a deal about it. He wasn't supposed to have them in the first place. Substitute one of his favorite toys instead.

He may keep going back to certain objects because they feel good on his gums and teeth, they appeal to his sense of smell, or he simply wants your attention. For his safety and your sanity, it's time to do two things: continue to work on the Drop it/Leave it command and to remove all temptation. You can also use the deterrent approach by spraying off-limits objects with Bitter Apple. Substitute rubber chew toys for the puppy to gnaw on, (again, those wet, frozen wash-cloths will help to relieve a puppy's mouth discomfort), spend some extra time with your pup, use distractions, and give him some additional mental and physical exercise. Your dog is most likely unclear about what items are acceptable or unacceptable when it comes to chewing, so be patient yet firm with him.

An older dog with a chewing habit can be more challenging. A teenage dog or an older adopted dog may be anxious, nervous, or stressed in his new surroundings. Your veterinarian should ascertain that there are no physical issues such as a bad tooth, sore gums, or a jaw injury. Changes in routine (including a new baby's arrival, new pets in the household, relocation, different surroundings) can stress your dog. Boredom can cause a dog to chew inappropriate objects as well.

As a puppy, Moxie was overly sensitive to changes in weather and would become extremely anxious when a thunderstorm was in the forecast. I learned to immediately do a quick search and rescue of all footwear before she chewed up my Reeboks.

Separation Anxiety

"All puppies have a difficult first few nights without their litter mates, but Berner puppies seem to be just heartbroken if they cannot be with you most of the time. I have had puppies with separation anxiety over just leaving them to go to work even. Please take their feelings and anxiety seriously. Once they bond with you, and they will quickly, all they want is to be with you."

MELINDA SUTTON
Beth's Bernies

There are few things that can tear your heart apart more than the sound of your dog crying as you're getting ready to leave him alone in the house. How does he even know that you're going out? Well, think about this: He has absolutely nothing better to do all day than to watch you. He knows your every move. Your Berner is a very smart and intuitive being, and he is usually aware of what you're going to do, even before you know. So, when he hears the sound of your house keys jingling in your coat pocket, or when he sees you putting on your running shoes to go out for some exercise, he knows you're about to leave. Welcome to the world of separation anxiety.

As if this phenomenon weren't difficult enough, researchers have recently found that several different forms of separation anxiety actually exist. One common type is a learned behavior. Does this routine sound familiar? You're getting ready to go to the supermarket, so you put your dog in his crate (if you are using one), put on your coat,

FUN FACT
Call of the Wild

In the early stages of animation for the 2020 *Call of the Wild* film, Buck, the film's canine star, was an animation based on a Bernese Mountain Dog. Unfortunately, this version of the dog didn't match the dog described by Jack London in his book, so the design was modified to resemble a mix between a Scotch Collie and St. Bernard.

and announce that you'll be back in a little while. "Be a good boy, I'll be right back!" Your dog knows exactly what happens next. He's memorized the words and motions that you use as you're going out the door. He's not at all happy. He knows that if he starts to cry, whimper, or bark, you'll run back over to comfort him, maybe offer him some treats, and you will give him plenty of attention. You try again to leave. Cue the barking and crying. You hesitate outside the door, wondering if the neighbors are calling the police to investigate a possible animal abuse case; your dog senses that you're still lurking outside, and the barking gets even louder.

I experienced this situation many years ago with my first dog, a very spoiled Cocker Spaniel named Sherman, so I know how agonizing it can be. Whenever Sherman was left alone, he would howl very loudly. (Picture a great big coyote howling at the full moon. That's what it sounded like.) I lived in a large apartment building at the time, so neighbors throughout the complex were quite aware that I'd gone out. If I went downstairs for five minutes to get the mail, Sherman would howl. If I left the apartment for two hours, Sherman would howl. Through no fault of my own, I earned the title of "That Woman".

I was miserable. Sherman was miserable. The neighbors were miserable.

Something had to be done quickly, or an eviction notice would be forthcoming. I assessed the situation and decided that my dog was both lonely and bored. I spent a small fortune on new toys for Sherman - chewy bones that I could fill with treats, fleecy dog toys, and everything on the pet store shelves that I thought would appeal to my pup. I put Sherman in his crate, gave him some of the newly purchased doggy toys, turned the radio on to my favorite classical music station for my dog's listening pleasure, and proceeded to totally ignore him as I left the house. There was not a sound to

Photo Courtesy
of Katie Walther

be heard from Sherman. Success! Everyone was happy, and "That Woman" was once again in the good graces of the neighbors. My method proved successful, but unfortunately, it's not always as easy for others whose dogs suffer from separation anxiety.

Sherman wasn't a bad dog. He wasn't nervous, anxious, or timid by any means. He was with me since he was three months old and purchased from a reputable breeder. He was a smart dog who, at an early age, grasped the concept of pushing Momma Dog's buttons. His separation anxiety was a learned behavior.

Learned behavior is only one of the causes of separation anxiety. If your dog is nervous or timid, has experienced changes in living arrangements, has a history of neglect, abuse, or abandonment, then separation anxiety should be considered very real and not something he's learned to do in order to get your attention. He is genuinely afraid to be alone.

Consider the dog who never lets his owners out of his sight. He follows them from room to room and panics when left alone. Even if a dog has never had the slightest reason to be fearful of being left alone, separation anxiety can, and often does, occur. Some breeds are more prone to this issue than others. Bernese Mountain Dogs are usually so thoroughly devoted to their human pack that becoming anxious when alone is a common reaction. Your best course of action is to be aware that it is, indeed, a possibility.

Your ultimate goal in easing separation anxiety is to instill confidence, independence, sociability in your dog, and to have a dog who understands that even though he'll be alone for a while, he has the assurance that you'll be returning. If your Berner is nervous when you leave the room, reinforce the Stay command with several short, fun, rewarding training sessions every day. Bring him into another room, tell him to "Stay", and leave him there for a few minutes. Walk back in, praise him, give him a treat, and some vigorous pats.

Gradually, extend the time you're away from your dog. You can also give him a toy to play with while he's away from you - something new or a tasty, stuffed, rubber bone to distract him and keep him occupied. When he starts to realize that being away from your side is not such a terrible thing, try this same process and leave the house. Don't make a fuss about leaving or returning. Your job is to simply ignore the dog. If he's typically in his crate when you leave, ask him to go into the crate, give him a toy or a treat (a high-value toy/treat works well here), and casually walk out of the house. If there's usually noise in the house when you are at home, leave the radio or television on to maintain the same atmosphere.

Another way to address separation anxiety is to alter your routine. Leave your car keys in the garage where the dog won't see or hear you pick them up. Wear a different jacket. Leave your purse at home. Change things up! Don't acknowledge that you're leaving. The less time your Berner has to work himself into a dither, the easier it will be to leave.

It's not necessary to wait until you're ready to leave before you offer that high-value toy or treat. Try giving it to him, hang out in the house for a few minutes while he's munching on his toy or stuffed bone, then exit without any fanfare. Don't even say goodbye. When you return, again, no big deal, no fussing over your fur baby. You're here, he's here, it's all good.

We always hope that the solution to a dog's separation anxiety will be uncomplicated, but sometimes, no matter how hard we try, it still doesn't work. A professional dog trainer who is familiar with this behavioral issue can be a valuable resource and can provide the necessary help. (Note: A trainer working with a separation-anxiety behavior will most likely need to work with you and your dog at your home for the best results.) Anti-anxiety medications for extreme separation issues are also available, so consult with your veterinarian for recommendations.

Digging

"To prevent your Berner from digging up the yard offer them their own digging box and encourage them to dig there by burying treats, bones, and toys and praising them for using their digging box. If they do dig a hole in the yard you can put some of their feces in the hole and cover it with dirt. It tends to deter them from digging up that same spot, but it could lead them to digging up another spot. If you consistently fill the holes this way they may eventually give up on digging all together."

ROBIN WORTS
Swiss Destiny Bernese Mountain Dogs

Bernese Mountain Dogs, like many other breeds, enjoy a good dig in your yard. In order to avoid having a formerly lovely backyard that soon resembles the craters of the moon, always supervise your dog when he's outside. A Berner will dig if he's bored, tired, hot, cold, hasn't had enough exercise, has had too much exercise, smells something interesting, needs a shady area in which to relax, or just because he's in the mood to dig. He'll bury his toys, your shrubs, your gardening tools. Unless you enjoy walking out to your yard and falling into an excavation pit that wasn't there yesterday, it's a good idea to keep reinforcing the Leave It command with your Berner. By saying, "Leave It," you're stating, "No Digging Allowed."

Another option is to provide the dog with a separate, acceptable spot where it's appropriate for him to dig to his heart's content. I roped off an area as a visual aid for my Berner, a notorious digger; I brought her over to that spot, took her big furry paws, and proceeded to help her dig. She quickly got the idea. When she "forgot" and went venturing off to a different area, I'd correct her and say, "Leave It", take her to her approved digging place and say, "Dig." She was happy to continue to excavate, and I got my yard back, minus the random holes.

You can also fill a sand box with soil or sand, bury some toys in it, and let her dig away. When left unsupervised, however, your Berner will not be terribly prudent in his archeological expeditions, and your garden may suffer the consequences.

Barking at the Door

I don't particularly mind that my dog considers herself an employee of my home security team. When someone rings our doorbell, it's her job to alert us that we have a visitor. She provides her services free of charge, and we never have to call for system maintenance. There are no electrical wiring or high-tech gadgets required. We can immediately silence the alarm by simply speaking the words, "No Barking."

However, not everyone is as lucky. Although most dogs consider it their duty to provide their human family with protection from strangers and to alert them when there's someone at the door, many dogs just don't know when to quit. A dog can't determine whom he should or shouldn't bark at, so he barks at everyone. He's just doing his job. Your job is to let him know when, if ever, his barking is appropriate.

It's time to add another command to your dog's vocabulary. Choose the words that you prefer to use but make them simple and use them consistently. "Quiet", "No barking", or "Stop" are all good options. At

Photo Courtesy of Kimberley Rice

my home, when someone I know or am expecting is at the door, I use my all-purpose word, "Friend" to let my dog know that everything is okay. It tells her that we're safe, she doesn't need to protect us, and we've got this. We're reinforcing the concept once again that she is not in charge, and her humans are the ones who make the decisions.

What's most important in training a dog not to bark at the door is remembering to keep your own response quiet, low-key, and calm. It's never acceptable to yell at your dog under any circumstances, especially when he's barking at the door. A loud voice reprimanding him will only serve to escalate the situation.

Some pet parents use spray bottles of water when the dog begins to bark. A stream of cold water to his backside is sometimes enough to get your point across. A soda can filled with pennies and shaken can also be used to redirect your dog's focus. If your dog is simply looking for attention, ignoring the barking altogether is another tactic.

Letting your guests know ahead of time that the dog may bark and asking them to ignore him is one more suggestion. However, these are all temporary solutions. Who wants to stand at the door with a spray bottle or soda can every time a guest visits? Good training, consistency, and positive reinforcement always offers the most permanent route to success. And remember this: There are times that you want your dog to bark at the door. Don't know who's ringing your door bell? Someone selling something? A shady looking stranger? If your dog hasn't heard your "friend" word, chances are pretty good that your undesirable visiter will beat a hasty retreat.

What's the best way to teach a dog the Quiet command? While it may seem odd, many trainers recommend that you train your dog to bark. Hold out a treat and say, "Speak." At some point, your dog will get the idea and bark. Praise him and give him the treat. Be consistent, patient, and positive. After he learns the Speak command, begin working on Quiet. He'll then get his treat when you give him the Quiet command and he complies. It sounds counterproductive and it may take a while, but your dog will get it eventually. If he doesn't, and he's become a non-stop barker, working with a professional dog trainer is the best solution. As with separation anxiety, it's most definitely recommended that you hire a trainer who will come to your home. This is a territorial issue; your dog needs to be protecting his own home in order for the training to be most effective.

Photo Courtesy of Lisa Gordon

Jumping

"Berners have a tendency to jump up on people. Start training 'Off' by teaching the puppy that it only gets attention or petting if all four feet are on the floor. You can also teach 'Up' so that your Berner can hug you but only when you ask for the behavior."

ANDREA CARLSON
Singing Sands Bernese Mountain Dogs

Bernese Mountain Dogs should never - let me repeat - NEVER - be allowed to jump on *anyone.* They're just too big, and their size can be the cause of a serious injury or a potential lawsuit. A jumping dog, no matter how friendly, displays a lack of good manners. It's rude, it's dangerous, and it can be frightening as well.

The most effective means to alleviate this behavior is to totally ignore the dog until all four of his paws are firmly on the floor. If your Berner insists on jumping on you as soon as you walk into the house, continue to walk past, and ignore him. Once he's settled down, you can praise him for his good behavior, give him a treat, or a gentle pat on the head. Remember to keep your demeanor calm and quiet and avoid exciting him. Speak to him in a quiet voice so he knows you're still happy to see him but let him know that a jumping dog will be ignored.

If your dog has a habit of jumping on your guests as they walk through the door, keep a collar and leash on him when visitors are expected. At the first sign of your Berner getting ready to jump, gently pull him back. Give him a firm and calm "No Jump" command. Once your dog settles down, your guests may calmly greet him. It's good to recruit a willing volunteer to practice working on this when company is NOT expected.

Bad habits can begin quickly in puppies. Teenage Bernese Mountain Dogs can develop poor etiquette as a means of garnering attention, coping with boredom, or simply testing to see how much will be tolerated. Older dogs may have come by their behavioral issues because previous owners just didn't know or care about the best way to remedy their dog's unpleasant habits. Have patience, let your dog know that you love him, and celebrate his successes, no matter how big or small they may be.

Aggression

Aggression issues are best left to a professional dog trainer or dog behavioral specialist. That's not to say that aggressive behavior can't be alleviated. Far from it. However, if you're seeing some tendencies toward growling, food possessiveness, territorial protectiveness, aggression while on leash, or dog fights (whether minor or more serious), then it is highly recommended that you consult with a professional dog-behavioral specialist.

Photo Courtesy of David and Anna Guilford

The cause of a dog's aggression can be the result of issues that are beyond your own dog training ability. Your Berner may be in pain and protecting himself from further injury. He may have been attacked or bullied by another dog or abused or neglected by a former owner. He may be fearful or protecting what he perceives as his territory. He could have actually been taught to be aggressive. Food aggression is thought to be the result of having to fight another dog for a share of a meal. Some dogs can show aggression when it comes to a favorite toy.

If you notice signs of aggression, then it's time to call in a specialist. It's a behavioral issue that can be remedied, but please don't wait until an injury - or worse - occurs. Aggression towards another dog or a human, should never be ignored, excused, or tolerated.

CHAPTER 17
The Health of Your Bernese Mountain Dog

Common Disorders and Health Concerns

"Berners are prone to many health issues, especially cancer, and have a shorter life span with an average age of death at eight years. Some can live longer and some can die early around four years of age."

ANDREA CARLSON
Singing Sands Bernese Mountain Dogs

Photo Courtesy
of Crizelle Ilejay

If you have acquired your Berner from a reputable, conscientious, and experienced breeder who strives to meet the criteria for excellence in their dogs, then your dog should, by all accounts, live a relatively long and healthy life. However, since Bernese Mountain Dogs are known to have a greater number of potential health problems than other breeds, this is something which anyone considering a Berner should keep in mind.

Some of the most common medical conditions seen in the Bernese Mountain Dog Breed are as follows:

FUN FACT
Kitty the Dog

The St. Regis Aspen Resort in the mountains of Colorado has adopted a new pet mascot, Kitty the Bernese Mountain Dog. Kitty Jacob Astor II is named after the founder of the St. Regis brand, John Jacob Astor IV, and his dog, Kitty. This sweet pup's duties include attending story-time, assisting with airport pickup, and welcoming guests. You can follow Kitty II's antics on Instagram (@ kittythebernese).

- **Malignant and systemic cancers,** with one of the most common being histiocytic sarcoma, which affects the cells of the immune system.

- **Hip dysplasia,** which is often hereditary, but can also be caused by environmental factors. Surgery is usually recommended, but non-surgical treatments such as physical therapy, glucosamine and nutritional supplements, and weight loss may also help.

- **Hypothyroidism,** a common disorder that is found in many breeds of dogs. Levothyroxine is the recommended treatment, administered by pills, which is required to be given to a dog every day throughout his entire life.

- **Elbow dysplasia,** a hereditary condition which affects the elbow joints. Surgery is usually the required treatment.

- **Kidney and liver disease,** which will affect these internal organs. Early diagnosis is essential in treating both conditions.

- **Von Willebrand Disease,** a hereditary disorder which affects blood clotting in Bernese Mountain Dogs. Since this disease is often seen in BMDs, a veterinarian may run diagnostic tests prior to any surgical procedure to be certain a dog is not a carrier of the VWB gene, which could potentially lead to excessive bleeding during surgery.

- **Bloat,** a gastric disorder, in which a dog's stomach distorts and fills with gas. Immediate surgical treatment is required as bloat can be fatal.

- **Parasites** are commonly found in dogs of all ages and particularly in young puppies. From walking outdoors in areas that are contaminated to fleas and ticks that are transmitted both indoors and outdoors, treatments are readily available but must be used diligently. A dog may reside in the cleanliest of environments, but even minimal contact with another pet who may be a carrier can result in an infestation. Fleas and ticks,

Photo Courtesy of Taylor Shoemaker

Photo Courtesy
of Amy Washenberger

ear mites, roundworms, hookworms, heart worm, and other parasites need to be treated as soon as possible to avoid further complications, including conditions which could prove to be fatal.

- **Arthritis** is a common ailment in older dogs and especially in larger breeds. A dog who suffers with pain and swelling in joints can be made more comfortable with the addition of joint supplements, dietary changes, moderate exercise, and avoidance of weight gain.

- **Allergies** are often seen in Bernese Mountain Dogs, so careful monitoring of a dog's behavior will be a good indication if something is amiss. Constant licking and scratching, head shaking, patchy spots on skin, discharge from the nose and eyes, sneezing, can all be signs that a Berner is suffering from an allergy. A dog may have a severe reaction to insect bites, such as bee stings, and although rare, vaccinations can also cause allergic reactions, which could be fatal.

- **Other disorders** seen in Berners include, but are not limited to, heart disease, epilepsy, cataracts, and other debilitating eye diseases.

The list may seem long and overwhelming to a new dog parent, but a little knowledge and a lot of preventative measures will go a long way to ensure that your Bernese Mountain Dog will remain healthy for many years to come.

Photo Courtesy
of Vinny Laracca

The Importance of Regular Veterinary Visits

We've discussed the importance of routine veterinary check-ups for your dog, and we've covered the value of following your veterinarian's advice regarding vaccinations, spaying/neutering, medications, and preventative measures. It's essential that any health concerns, no matter how minor they may appear at the onset, be addressed in a timely manner. Although the internet provides an abundance of information, please don't rely on it when it comes to the well-being of your Berner. Your dog's veterinarian should be your go-to source for all pertinent medical help. He or she has the expertise and the experience needed where your dog's health is concerned.

During a typical well-being or annual checkup, your veterinarian will discuss schedules for booster shots, vaccinations, laboratory work, spaying/neutering, testing for parasites, heart worm, flea and tick treatments, dental exams, and weight checks. You'll be asked about your Berner's daily routine, urinary and bowel schedules, and nutritional needs. Your dog's overall temperament, grooming, daily exercise and play times will be discussed, as well as training, general family and environmental details, day care, and socialization skills. Your veterinarian will want to hear your concerns and questions, so don't be afraid to ask. No question is too trivial!

If your new Berner is an older dog, your veterinarian will speak with you about many of the issues which apply to dogs of all ages, but there are other topics which should be addressed as well. Included in the discussion should be nutritional needs, orthopedic concern as they relate to an older dog's musculoskeletal structure, vitamin and dietary supplements, possible cognitive disorders, and any particular concerns that pertain to your aging Bernese.

Pet Insurance

There are pros and cons surrounding the need for pet insurance. Some pet parents view it as a necessity while others regard it as too costly an option, with limited coverage and restrictions. Here are some questions to ask when considering whether or not a policy fits your needs:

- What is the annual cost?
- What does the coverage include?
- What does the coverage NOT include?
- Have you researched what types of policies are offered by other companies?

Photo Courtesy
of Brittany Munster

- Does your veterinary practice accept the policy that you're considering?
- Is there a deductible?
- Are routine office visits and well-being visits covered?
- Is there an annual maximum coverage?
- Does the insurance cover pre-existing conditions?
- Is there coverage for accidents, emergency visits, chronic illnesses, and medications?
- Are on-going preventative medications, such as flea and tick and heart worm treatments, covered?
- What is the percentage of reimbursement?
- Do annual premiums increase as a dog ages?
- Are congenital and hereditary conditions covered?
- Is there coverage for surgery, laboratory testing, X-rays, ultrasounds, and scans?
- Are hospitalization and specialty referrals/care covered?
- Is there coverage for dental care, including cleaning and extractions?
- Is there coverage for alternative medical and therapeutic treatment?
- Is there a wait time before coverage begins?
- Must coverage start before the dog reaches a certain age?
- Is treatment for behavioral issues covered?
- Is there coverage for microchipping, prescription foods, and special diets?
- Are there discounts for multiple pets in the household?

You'll discover that annual costs and insurance coverage varies, depending on the company. Some homeowners' policies and automobile insurers may include pet insurance as a bundle feature, so be sure to check with your existing insurance companies to see if this is an option. One important aspect to think about if you decide to purchase pet insurance is that some companies do not deal directly with veterinarians, so you will be reimbursed at a later date. Whether or not you decide that pet insurance is something you'll need for your dog, remember that in the event of an accident or major illness, veterinary expenses can be exorbitant. No pet parent likes to think of the "what ifs" but planning ahead is an important investment for your dog.

CHAPTER 18
Your Bernese Mountain Dog's Nutrition

Whether you're a first-time pet parent or a seasoned dog owner, a casual stroll through the food aisle of your favorite pet store will probably be a confusing experience. So many choices! Should you purchase the canned food? Dry? Frozen? Freeze dried? Organic? Chicken? Fish? Beef? Venison? Are you ready to buy one of each, just in case your dog's discriminating taste buds don't approve of your selection? Which is healthier? This one has fillers! This one's got gluten! What's a pet parent to do? There's a simple solution: ASK!

Photo Courtesy of Jacquelyn Shipley

Keep it Consistent – Listen to Your Breeder

"We highly promote a high quality dry food ideal for fast growing Bernese. Feed a Bernese wrong and it'll either end up short and dumpy or tall and lanky, neither are very nice. Nature intends for a pup to look a certain way, by feeding a high quality kibble that pup will end up maturing as it should."

MRS. PHILIPPA GREEN

Pasturegreen Bernese Mountain Dog

If you've acquired your Berner puppy from a reputable breeder, your dog is already off to a good start by eating nutritious food which the breeder feels is an excellent source of proper ingredients on which his dogs thrive. The breeder will have the experience and knowledge to recommend the best foods for your dog, from puppyhood to maturity. You should also consult with your veterinarian; however, most veterinarians will likely suggest you continue to feed your dog the same food he was eating while at the breeder's. Unless there is a specific reason, such as food sensitivities or a health concern, it's recommended that you not make any changes at this stage of your puppy's development. Feeding times and amounts should be discussed with both your veterinarian and the breeder and followed carefully, according to their advice.

Large Breed Food

"Be aware that the amount of food he ate as an adolescent will be too much when he is fully grown. This is particularly true if the dog is spayed or neutered. There are way too many overweight Berners (or dogs in general)."

BARB WALTENBERRY
Barberry BMD

Photo Courtesy of Derek Gaffney

Large breed food for puppies is specially designed to give your new Berner all the daily requirements he needs, but can also ensure that your dog will not grow too quickly. Fast growth has been known to create muscle and skeletal problems in Bernese Mountain Dog puppies. Until your veterinarian recommends switching to the next age-appropriate food for your dog, it's important to keep him on puppy food - in most cases, at least throughout the first twelve months of his life.

Every dog's diet should include the proper balance of vitamins, minerals, carbohydrates, fats, and proteins for age, weight, and energy level. You'll need to modify amounts and feeding times as your dog matures. Any changes in his diet must be done on a very gradual basis. Your veterinarian and your breeder will have specific recommendations for your dog's nutritional requirements.

Mealtime Manners

Teaching your pup good manners around his food should be included in the overall training process. Ask your dog to Sit and Stay before the food bowl goes down and give him the OK command to go to his bowl. Some dogs are notorious chowhounds, and they can exhibit aggression while they're eating. This should never be tolerated. While your pup is enjoying his meal, place your hand near his food as he's eating. Speak calmly to him, tell him he's a good boy, and allow him to become accustomed to having someone near his food. Positively reinforcing your Berner's good dining etiquette at an early age will help to avoid potential problems later.

Vet Recommendations

You should also discuss your own personal preferences for your dog's nutrition with the breeder and veterinarian. Do you prefer a more holistic approach? Is your diet strictly vegetarian or vegan? You have the option of serving your dog home-cooked meals or raw foods, as many pet parents prefer to do, thus eliminating fillers, preservatives, and by-products. However, even though you may think your dog is eating a healthier, more nutritious diet, this may not be the case. The following are some of the food options to consider for your dog:

Dry, Large Breed Puppy Food – a.k.a. Kibble
This type of food makes feeding convenient, the price is reasonable, the food lasts a long time in the bag, and it can be purchased at most pet

stores. Concerns may center around a dog not consuming enough moisture/ liquid on a strictly dry dog food diet. (If this is an issue, water may be added to dry food.)

Wet Dog Food

Wet food is more expensive, and there could be more waste as canned food must be used quickly once it's opened. Some dogs will prefer wet food, so if your vet approves, canned food might better suit your picky dog's taste buds.

Photo Courtesy of Liz Smith

Raw and Home-Cooked Diets

"I am a Holistic Veterinarian and feel all pets do best with a species ap-propriate moisture rich diet. This would be a commercially balanced raw diet such as K9 kravings, Answers, Steve's, or Small Batch. Since Berners are prone to health issues including cancer and gut issues, raw diets are best to decrease in-flammation, prevent obesity, and provide good gut bacteria- the key to a healthy immune system! There is some current research in Berners showing increased longevity and less health issues when fed an appropriate diet."

ANDREA CARLSON
Singing Sands Bernese Mountain Dogs

There are many different opinions on whether a raw or home cooked diet is good for your dog. Yes, you'll know exactly what your dog is con-suming, as there are no fillers, chemicals, or preservatives. You'll also be spending a lot of time in the kitchen preparing food for your pooch. While it might sound like the perfect, healthy diet for your beloved Berner, there are some draw-backs: These types of diets are typically low in fat, and your dog needs some fat. Cost-wise, raw and home cooked meals will become quite expensive. Experts recommend that puppies, especially, should not be fed a raw/home cooked diet.

Feeding an Older Berner

When your dog is older, if you do decide that you want to feed him raw/home-cooked foods only, check with your vet for recommendations on the best diet for your dog. As he reaches maturity, your dog's diet and caloric intake may need to be adjusted depending upon his energy level and any health concerns. He may develop allergies, digestive issues, or musculoskel-etal disorders. He may need more vitamins, protein, and more or less fats or fiber. Your own dietary preference might be gluten-free, but your veterinar-ian may suggest otherwise for your dog. Your Berner may suddenly decide, for whatever reason, that he's just not all that interested in the food that he's been eating for the past few years. No matter which food you choose for your dog, be sure the ingredients will provide him with a nutritionally complete and balanced diet.

For pet parents of an older dog, at some point, you should consider whether you're feeding your dog the same foods and amounts that you always did. Is he getting fat? Obesity is a common cause of many conditions

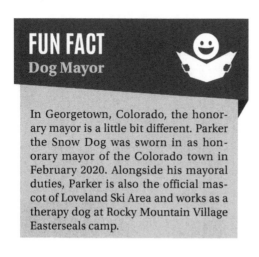

that can be prevented, so discuss possible changes in your dog's nutrition and dietary requirements with your veterinarian. If your Berner is leading a more sedate lifestyle, adjustments in his food intake might be necessary. Between-meal snacks of store-bought treats can be substituted with vegetables that your dog finds appetizing, such as cooked carrots. Inexpensive dehydrators can produce a limitless number of nutritious snacks that taste like crunchy, jerky-style treats by using chicken, turkey, or fish. Dried apple, sweet potato slices, and dehydrated banana slices might appeal to the Berner with the fussiest palate. Health-minded, cost-conscious pet parents can score a big win with their dog, as well as their wallet, by implementing a few innovative, home-made snacks.

Foods to Avoid

In Chapter 3, Preparing for Your New Dog's Arrival, we touched on foods that should never be given to your Berner. He'll undoubtedly love whatever his humans are eating, but not all people food will be good for him. Those big, sad eyes will melt your heart as he begs for a smidgeon of your food. Resist all temptation to share the following items with your pooch:

- Tomatoes
- Avocado
- Bones that can splinter, including beef, fish, and chicken
- Citrus fruits
- Onions
- Garlic
- Chocolate
- Raisins
- Grapes
- Nuts
- Caffeine
- Bread dough
- Coconuts
- Chewing gum (and other items containing xylitol)
- Alcohol.

There are many recipes available online and in specialized dog-recipe cookbooks geared toward homemade dog foods and treats. All food and treats should initially be given to your dog in moderation to avoid stomach upsets, digestive issues, or allergic reactions.

Probiotics for Dogs

"I think no matter what food you feed a good Probiotic/Prebiotic/ Digestive Enzyme supplement is a must have. A healthy gut is the first step to raising a healthy dog!"

ROBIN WORTS
Swiss Destiny Bernese Mountain Dogs

Some veterinarians now recommend a probiotic supplement for dogs if there are concerns regarding digestive issues. My rescue dog, healthy in most respects, had occasional bouts of intestinal upheaval. Every once in a while, for no apparent reason, she would experience intestinal distress in the form of diarrhea or constipation. After routine testing which had normal results, my veterinarian recommended a daily dose of a probiotic. This was approximately three years ago, and she has not had another occurrence of digestive upset since.

It must be noted that probiotic supplements should not be given to puppies or to dogs with severely compromised immune systems. Probiotics for humans should never be given to a dog. Although at this time, there is still no conclusive research findings as to the benefits of dog probiotics, many have found that dogs with digestive issues, skin allergies, bad breath, and excessive gas will experience some symptomatic relief.

Photo Courtesy of Laura Orsini

CHAPTER 19
Grooming Requirements

"Berners have a LOT of it and it doesn't all stay attached to the dog. They shed a little bit all the time and a LOT several times a year. You'll need to brush your dog quite often and bathe him periodically. Some owners like to bathe and groom their dogs and others prefer to take them to a groomer. If you are the latter, you might want to price grooming in your area and factor that in when considering a Berner."

BARB WALTENBERRY
Barberry BMD

Photo Courtesy
of Vicki L. Mayer

Every Bernese Mountain Dog owner will have their own methods when it comes to dog grooming, and every professional groomer will have their own way of doing things. So how does a new Berner owner decide which grooming process will work best? A good place to start is with your Berner's breeder if you have one. They've likely been grooming their dogs for many years and are knowledgeable as to grooming requirements, procedures, and frequency.

Not all Berners have the same type of coat. Some may be silky, others coarse. Some are wavy, others stick-straight. All Berners shed...and shed... and shed some more. With proper equipment and a regular grooming schedule, you'll be able to stay ahead of the game.

Hiring a Professional Groomer

"Get your dog familiar with visiting a professional groomer when they are young. They have a lot to learn when it comes to tolerating grooming and if they start off young when they are smaller it will be easier on everyone and easier on your pocketbook down the road."

ROBIN WORTS
Swiss Destiny Bernese Mountain Dogs

Start as early as possible to get your dog accustomed to being groomed. In addition to speaking with your breeder for advice, consult with a groomer who is familiar with the BMD breed and their specific traits. Some Berners have allergies and skin sensitivities, so professional groomers would need to use appropriate methods, products, and equipment. Interviewing a potential groomer ahead of time will help in selecting one with whom you can easily discuss everyone's expectations. Some questions to ask a groomer and observations you should make when interviewing are as follows:

- Is the facility clean?
- Have you had experience grooming Bernese Mountain Dogs?
- What is the cost, and what is included?
- Do you have liability insurance?
- How long will I need to leave my dog?
- Do you work alone, or do you have assistants?

- Are you certified or licensed by the state? (Note: Every state has different requirements. Check to see whether there is licensing or certification in your state or if certain educational standards must be met.)
- What type of products do you use? (If your dog has allergies, you will need to be sure that appropriate care is taken.)
- How many dogs are in the facility at one time?
- Are the dogs closely supervised while in your facility?
- Are the dogs crated, and do they get potty breaks?
- How often do you recommend my dog be professionally groomed?
- Can you show me the best way to groom my dog between visits?
- Do you have references?

After you've selected a groomer, it may take a few sessions before everyone is on board with what needs to be done. Give your Berner's new groomer a chance to work with you and your dog. Explain your expectations clearly and concisely and ask for their professional opinion. If you're happy with the results, tip them well. They'll appreciate your confidence in their work.

Photo Courtesy
of David and Anna Guilford

Grooming Your BMD at Home

"The Bernese has a beautiful coat when cared for properly. One tip that was told to me early on is to brush from the tail to the head. It sounds strange but it works!"

DIANE CALDEMEYER REID
Faraway Farms Inc.

Although Berners might look like they're high maintenance dogs, with some regular effort on your part, the grooming process should be fairly straightforward. Be sure to have the right equipment on hand. Here are the basic supplies that you'll need, although your groomer may suggest additional tools:

- Brushes and combs (A stainless-steel pin brush works best)
- Detangling dog shampoo
- Detangling spray
- Ear cleaner
- Scissors
- Cotton balls
- Dental cleaning supplies
- Nail clipper or Dremel grinder
- Styptic powder
- Cool air circulating or low-heat dryer

Don't Over Bathe

"Buy a blower. I have a powerful livestock blower called a Circuiteer. If you do not dry them completely, they are prone to hotspots."

GIGI RAYMOND
Rhapsody BMDS

Berners often have dry skin, so it's not recommended that you bathe your dog too frequently - once a month should be enough, unless he's been rolling in the mud or some other unseemly substance. Berners have double coats, so be diligent about giving your dog a thorough, deep brushing. Twice a week is optimal, but a once-a-week session will suffice, as long as it's done correctly. Berners shed constantly, but when the weather changes, shedding increases. If your home is covered with doggy tumbleweeds, get that brush out and get working!

Fur Mats and Tangles

"Shaving a Berner is NOT going to help them keep cool. It actually does the opposite and is damaging to their coats. Their coats insulate them from heat and cold."

AMY KESSLER
Lionheart Bernese

Some Bernese Mountain Dogs are prone to fur mats and tangles so keep detangling spray handy. Mats can then be worked through gently with a comb. Be sure to check your dog carefully during each grooming session and watch for areas that are common for mats to appear - behind your dog's ears, under his tail, on his chest, near his armpits, and on his underside. If you're confident using scissors around your dog, you can shape the fur on his paws, trim fur around his ears, and tidy up his foot pads. If you're planning to bathe your Berner, brush him first. Tangles are much easier to remove when the dog is dry, and there will be less hair going down the tub's drain. A thorough drying, with either absorbent towels or a cool, dog-safe hair dryer, is essential.

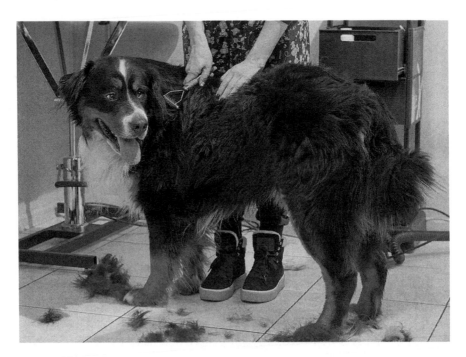

Photo Courtesy
of Rhona Eklund

Cleaning the Ears

Pay careful attention to areas in and around your dog's ears. When wet, a Berner's floppy ears can trap moisture inside, thus allowing for bacterial growth and potential ear infections. Use cotton balls or a soft washcloth to carefully dry any water or dampness. Never...EVER...use a cotton swab on your dog's ears! Even if you're not bathing your dog, check his ears during regular grooming sessions, and if you detect any odor, wetness, or redness, schedule an appointment with your vet.

Berner Teeth Brushing

A dog's teeth should be brushed several times a week, and should be started at an early age. It will keep his breath smelling sweet, and you'll also be sure that dental decay and neglect will not be contributing factors to potential health problems. Poor oral hygiene can cause bacteria, which in turn can affect your dog's digestive system as well as his internal organs. Too many dogs undergo costly and painful teeth extractions and suffer from periodontal disease due to a lapse in brushing their teeth.

FUN FACT
Presidential Pets

Irish President Michael D. Higgins is a renowned dog lover. He owns two Bernese Mountain Dogs who are often seen with him during his daily affairs. Síoda and Bród are such a fixture in the life and affairs of President Higgins that people have been known to inquire after the dogs when Higgins appears without them.

To brush your dog's teeth, you'll need a dog toothbrush, which is curved and has a longer handle that can easily reach your dog's back teeth. You'll also need some dog toothpaste. Both of these items are available in pet supply stores as well as online. Do not use toothpaste made for humans as it could contain ingredients that are toxic for your pet.

Try to set up a regular time and place to brush your dog's teeth. Choose a quiet, well-lit location and a time when there are no interruptions to allow you and your dog to focus on the process at hand. Be gentle and introduce your dog to having his muzzle handled and his teeth brushed in a manner that's calming for him and calming for you. If you're nervous, he will quickly read those signals you're sending as something to fear.

To begin, put a dab of the toothpaste on your finger and encourage your dog to taste it. Most dogs find the flavor acceptable. Now add the toothpaste to the brush and begin to gently brush his top front teeth while holding his upper lip out a bit. Move on to the sides of his upper teeth, proceed to the bottom (don't forget the inner sections of the teeth), and that's it! Don't forget to praise your dog as you're brushing. He may not love having his teeth brushed initially, but with a regular routine, encouragement for his excellent behavior, and your own relaxing demeanor, he'll soon become accustomed to the procedure. He may even enjoy it!

Photo Courtesy
of Mindy Harrison

Nail Clipping

Attention to your dog's nails is another important aspect of his overall grooming requirements. If you choose to clip your dog's nails yourself, it should be done approximately once a month. A Berner who spends most of his time walking on grass and softer surfaces, as opposed to concrete or asphalt, may need to have his nails clipped more often; sidewalks and streets will wear down a dog's nails more quickly than soft surfaces. If you have no experience with canine nail clipping, it's highly recommended that you ask your dog's groomer or veterinarian for a how-to demonstration.

Here's my (slightly embarrassing) true confession: I am proud to say that I have no qualms about wielding a heavy chain saw and deftly and confidently removing limbs from a tree. I am the relative who's called upon every Thanksgiving to expertly carve the turkey. I can perform a professional-grade manicure and pedicure on myself. But when it comes to clipping my dog's nails, I'm terrified. If you, too, decide that it's something you'd rather not do, your dog's groomer, veterinarian, or a qualified doggy day-care staff member will be happy to do the job. The cost is minimal (usually included in regular grooming appointment services), and honestly, if you're not comfortable holding a scissors-type nail clipper or a Dremel grinder in the vicinity of your pooch's precious paws, it's best to leave it to the experts. If you're confident that you can do the job yourself, we would highly recommend following instructions provided by your dog's caring professionals. Internet research will also offer a wealth of information as well as excellent how-to videos on the nail clipping process. Sites such as ASPCA.org and BMDCA.org are extremely helpful.

Checking for Parasites and Skin Concerns

As part of his regular grooming routine, be sure to check your dog daily for fleas and ticks and be on the lookout for any signs of these nasty little buggers. They will burrow their way into your dog's skin, and because of his dark coat, they may go unnoticed. A thorough inspection, especially during tick season and in warm climates, should be done whenever your dog has been in grassy or wooded areas or around other dogs. Fleas and ticks can jump from one dog to another quite easily, and many a dog has stepped on a tick nest, so inspect his paws as well. When you're out for a walk with your dog, carry tweezers with you for an emergency tick removal. Don't wait until you're back in the house to look for for any freeloading insects. Better to discover them before you're indoors and save the cost (and agony) of a home debugging!

Baths, bug inspections, nail clippings, ear cleaning, brushings, dental hygiene, dematting - admittedly, there is work involved in keeping your Berner looking and feeling his healthy best. However, when started at an early age, done with love, and with lots of cuddles and praise, these tasks can also be an amazing bonding experience for you and your dog – and what's better than that?

Photo Courtesy
of Laurie Pinchuk

CHAPTER 20

Your Aging Bernese Mountain Dog

"In Berners, there is a saying: '3 years a puppy, 3 years a good dog, and 3 years an old dog'. The best advice for your senior Berner is to have them checked by a veterinarian and run lab work every 6 months. If you find any lumps, they should be checked immediately by a vet and if your Berner seems off at all, don't wait for a vet check up."

ANDREA CARLSON
Singing Sands Bernese Mountain Dogs

Photo Courtesy
of Sarah Fay

Photo Courtesy
of Brittany Christner

How quickly the time passes! One day, you're reveling in that new puppy smell of your soft, pudgy little Berner. You're amazed at how quickly he's learned to sit and stay, and he's become your loyal, beloved companion in the blink of an eye. There were trials and tribulations along the way - the "fun" of potty training and that awful cone that he begrudgingly sported after his neutering. It took a while before he understood that the cat was not put on this earth simply for his amusement. As he matured, things began to settle in nicely, and he loved nothing better than a good game of fetch-the-tennis-ball, followed by a long nap. His social skills made him a member in good standing at doggy day care, and the neighbors carried a pocketful of treats just in case your big Berner was passing by.

Or are you thinking back to the day you adopted a sad-looking Berner who was being fostered by that nice family? Do you remember how you saw his picture online, read his sorrowful history of neglect, and decided, with some trepidation, that you were up for the challenge of making his senior years a little happier? What a wonderful job you've done...he's living his best life, just a little less actively these days. Give yourself a pat on the back. You've got the admiration of Bernese lovers everywhere.

No matter when or where you first met and fell in love with your Bernese Mountain Dog, the years since have been filled with an abundance of wonderful memories; at some point, you'll notice that your furry pal is showing signs of slowing down. It may be a gradual process. He is becoming somewhat lethargic, his energy level is decreasing, he is developing some lumps and bumps on his skin where there were none previously, and his mobility is not what it once was.

Life Expectancy, Aging, and Vet Care

SAYING GOODBYE
Bella Gellar

Sarah Michelle Gellar, star of the popular TV series *Buffy the Vampire Slayer*, had to say goodbye to her beloved Bernese Mountain Dog, Bella, after six years together. In a memorial Instagram post to Bella, Gellar said, "And while I don't think six years with you was nearly enough, I'm grateful to have had you in my life."

With the breed's shortened life expectancy, your Berner can be considered a senior citizen at the age of seven. The good news is that with early intervention and new medical treatments, Berners are living longer now than in recent years. Adjustments will be necessary as your dog ages; some may be minor while others more considerable.

Routine veterinary visits should be an essential part of your dog's physical and mental health as he grows older. Medications and supplements that are recommended by your veterinarian can prolong your dog's life and could mean the difference between continued good health or unnecessary discomfort for your Bernese Mountain Dog.

As all dogs age, no matter the breed, they are prone to various disorders and illnesses, even more so for the Bernese. Some common ailments include:

Photo Courtesy of David and Anna Guilford

Arthritis

Your dog's genetics, environment, nutrition, exercise, and weight all play a role in his aging process, especially when it comes to his bones and joints. Just as people experience stiffness and soreness in their limbs as they grow older, the same is true with dogs.

Cataracts

As your dog ages, you may notice that his eyes have developed a whitish coating. It's most likely due to cataracts, and it usually affects both eyes, although not always at the same time. A certified veterinary ophthalmologist should be consulted to determine whether surgery is an option.

Urinary Incontinence

There are many reasons why your dog may be unable to hold his urine during his senior years. It's usually more common in female dogs, but it can happen to male dogs as well. Possible reasons for incontinence in Berners include hormonal imbalance, urinary tract infections, kidney problems, and bladder infections. Neurological issues, urethral disorders, congenital defects, spinal injuries, and degenerative ailments may also need to be considered. With testing, your veterinarian will be able to determine the cause of your dog's incontinence. Depending upon the cause, he or she can advise on the best way to treat the disorder, often without surgery.

Canine Cognitive Dysfunction

(CCD) is comparable to Alzheimer's disease or dementia in humans. Your dog may experience changes in his behavior such as sleeping more or less than usual, an increase or decrease in appetite, confusion, overall lethargy, little interest in daily routine, forgetfulness, and potty accidents. Although medical research has recently offered some hope with scientific trials, there is still no definitive cure. Various medications, supplements, and herbal treatments may give your senior Berner some relief from the symptoms of this disease, so consult with your veterinarian.

Photo Courtesy of Dylan Stewart

Hypothyroidism:

*Photo Courtesy
of Laurie Pinchuk*

Many older and senior Bernese Mountain Dogs are diagnosed with thyroid issues which present with weight fluctuations, excessive thirst, a dull coat, hair loss, patchy dry skin, and lethargy. Your veterinarian will diagnose a thyroid issue by administering a blood test and if positive, will likely prescribe a daily dose of medication for your Berner.

Other diseases which appear with some frequency in senior Bernese Mountain dogs include obesity, allergies, high blood pressure, heart disease, liver, kidney and blood disorders, autoimmune disorders, dental disease, and various cancers. Be aware of any changes that you're observing in your dog. Whether you perceive it as an emergency or just something a bit out of the ordinary, keep your veterinarian informed of anything that just doesn't seem right.

Keeping Your Senior Berner Active

Even though your dog may be slowing down, keeping him active is still important. Daily walks, indoor and outdoor playtime, and socialization may need to be scaled back, with moderation being the key factor. Check with your veterinarian for advice on what and how much activity your dog can tolerate. Low impact exercise, swimming, or even a walk-in shallow water will benefit dogs with osteoarthritis.

Besides physical exercise, your dog will also have a need for mental stimulation. He'll still love a game of hide-the-treats, interactive toys, and short, gentle walks to new places where he can experience unfamiliar sights, sounds, and scents.

Therapeutic measures have been shown to aid with some senior dogs' health concerns. Depending upon your dog's individual needs, massage, hydro/water therapy, Reiki, acupressure and acupuncture, chiropractic treatment, laser therapy, and physical therapy may be advised.

Photo Courtesy
of Shelby Brooks

Photo Courtesy
of Liz Smith

Simple Adjustments for an Older Dog

"I've had very good luck with keeping a harness and belly strap on my older Berners. When they struggle to get up, it's easy to lift them onto their feet. I've also used dog boots for improved traction while walking- huge help. Also, use a ramp into your vehicle."

BARB WALTENBERRY
Barberry BMD

Foregoing additional calories might seem like an obvious change that will give your senior Bernese Mountain Dog an advantage when it comes to a healthier lifestyle. What other signs should you be looking for that will help make your senior dog's life a little easier? Is he sleeping more on the living room carpet, where once he preferred to leap up onto the sofa? Does he hesitate to get into the car? He may be trying to tell you that his legs are stiff, and it's an awful lot of effort to make that jump even if it does mean a ride to the ice cream shop for a doggy treat.

A car ramp is a great accessory to help your Berner with mobility issues. They're easy to transport, fold quickly for tucking away in the car's rear hatch or trunk, are lightweight, and your dog will be able to continue to enjoy his car rides. The ramps are sold with non-slip surfaces and many are adjustable for vehicle or sofa height.

Your dog's favorite sleeping spot can be made more accessible to him with an orthopedic bed. Stair climbing may be difficult for a dog with arthritic joints, so consider providing a comfortable bed for him on your home's first floor. Orthopedic dog beds will add extra support for his spine as well as decrease stress points on his joints and bones. Before purchasing a bed, always consider how the dog sleeps - on his side or stomach? Stretched out or curled up in a ball? Bolster pillow or flat bed? Your senior dog is sleeping longer hours now, so he would lovingly appreciate a nice, comfy spot to rest those weary bones.

Physical Changes

Berner parents often notice that their senior dog's skin will undergo some changes. You may discover new bumps on your dog - fatty tumors, warts, cysts, lesions, and growths are common. Itchy, dry skin and a coat that becomes easily matted or dull can be the result of allergies or vita-min deficiencies. Many of these skin changes are harmless and benign, but early detection of a potential health concern and a visit to the veterinarian is always the best course of action. With careful inspection and regular grooming sessions, you'll be aware of any new skin problems that need attention.

Senior dogs may exhibit behavioral changes. Let's think about this: If your back is bothering you, or you've been awake all night tossing and turning because your arthritis is kicking up, you're probably not going to be on top of your game the following day. It's the same with your older dog. If your usually sweet and gentle Berner is acting grumpy, it may be due to physical discomfort. Is he not listening to you? His hearing may be compromised. His potty accidents could be the result of urinary incontinence, and he may demonstrate some confusion in his daily routine, including forgetting commands. Your Berner's appetite could change as well - either increasing or

Photo Courtesy of Molly Zingler

decreasing. He might be restless, anxious, more fearful. Where he was once thrilled to be outside in the cold, perhaps he's now happier to sit and snuggle in front of the fireplace. Likewise, on a steamy, hot day, your dog might prefer to relax in an air-conditioned room or enjoy hanging out in a kiddie pool outside in a shady spot.

It's difficult to watch our beautiful Berners slow down, but it's up to us, as the guardians of our furry kids' health and well-being, to make them as comfortable as we possibly can. It's all part of their natural aging process, so love your Berner, help him through these challenging times, and enjoy every moment with your beloved dog.

When it's Time to Say Good-bye

"Treasure every moment and every year. Berners teach you to be present in the moment, as we only have them for a short while."

DANIEL MERCER
Mermac Kennel

You've done your best for your dog since the day you first met him. You've provided him with love and friendship, nourished him, kept him healthy, and given him a good life. Sadly, there comes a time when you will know that you must say goodbye. It's heartbreaking.

Be realistic as you assess the quality of your dog's life. Is he no longer eating, drinking, or able to stand and walk? Is his body functioning as it should? Has he been injured, or has he deteriorated to the point where it's unlikely that he will recover? Just as you planned for your new dog's arrival, this again is the time to prepare. And just as you've discussed your Berner's needs with your veterinarian as you accompanied your dog through the many stages of his life, your vet will be there to guide you now as well.

He or she is a compassionate, caring professional who understands what you are experiencing now; they will be there to offer help and advice in every way possible once you've made the decision that euthanasia is the only option. It certainly won't make things easier, but you may find a bit of solace in knowing that the word euthanasia comes from the Greek words meaning gentle and easy death.

Depending upon the circumstances, some veterinarians will offer to come to a patient's home to euthanize. It's something that should not only be discussed with your pet's doctor but also with your household members. Sometimes a clinical setting, as opposed to a home setting, is a better choice.

You'll need to be prepared to make other decisions. Will you want to be there with your dog as you say a final farewell? We want our dogs to know that we're with them, comforting them until the end, but some pet parents may find it much harder to be present. It's a decision that only you can make. Listen to your heart.

In most cases, a veterinarian will administer a sedative to your dog before giving an injection of pentobarbital, which will cause the heart to slow down, and ultimately, stop beating. Your beloved Berner will be at peace. The veterinarian will discuss post-euthanasia arrangements with you - choices you will need to make which will be the most comforting for you and your family, such as cremation and burial.

As you grieve the passing of your pet, you should know that there are support groups available as well as individual counseling programs to help during this time. Your veterinarian may have resources available. There are also online sites which will assist in finding help, including some state university programs dedicated to coping with pet loss. Those who have ever loved and lost a pet will understand the sadness you're experiencing. Reach out to others. You are not alone.

Everyone grieves the loss of a pet differently. I've had to go through this many, many (too many) times throughout my life. As my heart recovers, I know that sooner or later, well-meaning friends and family will inevitably ask, "So, when are you going to get another dog?" There's no easy answer. They are trying to be kind and well-meaning, but only you will know when - and if - the time is right. For me, personally, I've always reached the decision as I process the grief and begin to sort through my memories of the many happy hours I've spent with my dog.

I think about the cute-as-a-button pooch who never failed to make me smile as I watched her play her puppy games. I remember the frustration I felt as she endlessly annoyed me with her teenage rebelliousness. Even as I arrived home to the sight of a roll of toilet tissue strewn throughout the house or my good leather purse devoured, I looked beyond it to her utter cuteness. As I sat and watched her cuddle with hospital patients who were in desperate need of some comfort, I knew that I would always be thankful for our time together. I missed that happy puppy face, those slobbering doggy kisses, the wagging tail that greeted me upon my return home every night. I missed the body language that said, "Hey, where have you been? I thought you'd never get home!" I missed my best friend. My house was empty, my heart was empty. I remembered one of my favorite quotes - from A.A. Milne's Winnie the Pooh:

"How lucky I am to have something that makes saying goodbye so hard."

I was indeed lucky, but now I needed to start all over. It was the right time.

So, a new chapter in my life began. I rescued a four-month-old puppy from Georgia. Her joyful demeanor belied her sorrowful history. She was abandoned and left by the side of a road to survive on her own. She was suffering from a parasitic infestation that would have killed a dog lacking her spirit and will to live. Thanks to a caring foster family, she was nursed back to health and made the journey north to a local animal shelter where I met her and instantly fell in love with my new pup.

We're a family again. We take long walks, we play, we snuggle, and we find comfort in just "being". We've come full circle. Life is good.

****

The Beginning

There'll be ups and downs,

But mostly ups.

Just look at those chubby and sweet Bernese pups!

Or that sad, older Berner, in need of a home,

With a story to tell, of surviving alone.

No matter the history, just open your heart,

As your Berner adventure,

Is about to start.

Take all your worries and cast them aside,

Buckle your seatbelt, it'll be quite a ride!

Here's why we love them,

Please keep this in mind:

Each Berner's unique,

Surely one of a kind.

They're big and they're furry,

Goofy, yet wise,

The original lap dog,

With an extra-large size.

White tip on his tail,

White blaze on his face.

His walk is a mixture,

Of clumsy and grace.

A beautiful dog,

He's sure to turn heads,

With a coat that is perfect,

Except when it sheds.

Sociable, loving, your family he'll guard,

When he's not excavating,

Huge holes in your yard.

Part angel, part devil,

Full of mischief and sass,

He'll be an "A" student,

In his dog-training class.

Curious and smart,

He's quite a quick learner.

There's no dog on earth,

That compares to a Berner.

Devoted and loyal,

His love has no end.

You'll soon understand,

He's indeed your best friend.

He'll romp in the snow,

And then sleep like a log.

Just a few reasons to love,

A Bernese Mountain Dog.

This book is dedicated to
My sweet Berner girl,
Moxie, the Wonder Dog